SINGING AN EPIC OF PEACE

a Fifth World Story-Poem

Appliable to Worlds Both Inner and Outer

Written with various verse forms
and with brush calligraphy and illustrations

by
Walter E. Harris III

Allbook Books
Hauppauge, N.Y., United States of America

Published by: Allbook Books

— PO Box 562
Selden, NY 11784

ISBN 0-9743603-0-9

COVER ART SYMBOLS

TOP:
From ancient Egypt: ATEN'S DISK—
a Solar disk with extending rays (arms with hands.) The Sun is
'born' each day, nourishes the Earth, and shines on all.

LEFT:
This TURTLE is a composite of turtle-shapes chosen from various
cultures that have some connection with the 'symbolic colors or
Races'. The associations of direction and elements vary with
cultures and traditions.

The Black Race (African), associated with the direction West,
element Water—
    (shell-shape of an ancient Egyptian river turtle.)

The White Race (Anglo/European), associated with the North,
element Fire—
    (the text-book drawing of a turtle's head.)

The Red Race (American Indian), associated with the East,
element Earth—
    (an Hawaiian sea turtle's front arms, from petroglyphs.)

The (Yellow) or Gold Race (Asian), associated with the South,
element Air—
    (ancient Chinese pictograph of quartered shell-grid - Tortoise)

This Whole-Turtle portrays the Four colors of the 'primary' or
'symbolic' Races, as well as the natural progression of Alchemy—
Black to White to Red to Gold.)

RIGHT:
Ancient Chinese pictograph:
                    Bird (above) + Mountain (below) = ISLAND

A "Bird" resting on a "Mountain" (or rock on the Ocean,)
thus represents the word "Island".

As souls we are able to fly anywhere, yet in human form, we
make our home on Earth, or as American Indian lore and other
world mythologies say: TURTLE ISLAND.

MANY THANKS TO:
The 'Tree' - for bearing and sharing its fruit
"I Ching" - *Kuei-Shan Ye Jinn* - for guidance
the Internet and WorldWideWeb - for making research much easier
Kay - for urging me to write again
Barbara - for listening, sharing and many, many comments...
The Sagency - for encouragement, links, comments....
Jeffrey - for enjoying the 'Turtle'
Ali - for understanding the calligraphy...at first glance
Mark & Patti - for encouragement
Judy - for encouragement
Ed - for very helpful suggestions
Richard G. - for comments and links
Susan - for printer suggestion
Emma, a 'Brit' - for info on the "Virgin" Queen
Maxwell - for mentioning Red Jacket
Jay - for his journey
Malcolm - for writing "ad astra per aspera"
John - for the Bear & Flute story
Jim "Bip" - for the 'Moose' and respect for 'history'
Terry - for computer help and humor
Keith & Sharon - for encouragement and computer help
Shawn, and Singh-Kaur - for comfortable space
James - for some information on 'the beat poets'
Joseph - for (r)evolution
Richard S. - for comments on the covers, front and back
the folks at N. B. - for their encouragement
Performance Poets Association™ and fellow poets & friends -
    for a supportive community and a place to share poetry
Deep Arrow Woman - for being a 'sister'
Tim, Mike, Tonia, Marge, Ron & others - for technical advice

&

this book is for.....

— that one lonely person seeking a way —

"Tell me, muse, of the story-teller...
...who was thrust to the edge of the world...
...childlike, ancient...
...and through him...
...reveal Everyman...

"The world seems to be sinking into dusk but I tell the stories as in the beginning, in my sing-song voice, which sustains me, protected by the tale from the troubling present, and protected for the future....

"My heroes are no longer the warriors and kings, but the things of peace, each equally good. The drying onions being equal to the tree-trunk that guides through the marsh...

"But so far no one has succeeded in singing an epic of peace. What is it about peace... that keeps its inspiration from enduring and makes it almost untellable? Should I now give up? If I do give up, mankind will lose its story-teller. And once mankind loses its story-teller, then it will have lost its childhood....

"I will not give up...

"Where are my heroes? Where are you, my children? Where are my own, the dull-witted, the first, the original ones?"

The old man/story-teller/spiritual guide
in Wim Wenders' film "Wings of Desire"

WARNING:
This poem may transform your perspective and viewpoints... and also contains minimal amounts of sexually graphic imagery.

TABLE OF CONTENTS

- Title page   i
- Cover Art Symbols   iii
- Quote page   v
- Table of Contents pages   vi
- Introductory Notes   ix

SINGING AN EPIC OF PEACE
- Peace pictograph   1
- Proem   2

BOOK 1 – RADIANT ILLUMINATION
PART 1 – THE YEAR OF RADIANT ILLUMINATION   3
- Spring   4
- Summer   13
- Autumn   19
- Winter   25
- Cycle of Seasons   32

PART 2 – AWAKENINGS   33
- And So
- Walking the Path   34
- Brothers   35
- Sisters
- Songs: Sound and Silence   36

PART 3 – BLESSINGS   39
- THERE but for the Grace of God
- A Prayer Between Here and Now   40
- "Facing a moment of..."   41
- Lady and Man Who Reads This   42

BOOK 2 – TURTLE ISLAND   44
PART 1 – THE BALLAD OF TURTLE ISLAND (NORTH AMERICA) 47
- Turtle Island   49
- Pre-Amble, or, Those Who Walked Before   55
- The State of the States of the Union   59
- 1) Of Water (mostly)
         Delaware – The Grandfathers; Washington – "The Father";
         Mississippi – "The Other Father"; Michigan; Missouri; Nebraska;
         Tennessee; Ohio; Kentucky; Connecticut; Minnesota; Wisconsin;
         Oregon; Idaho; Arizona.

- 2) Of Air & Allies (mostly)   80
    Kansas; Arkansas; Oklahoma; North and South Dakota; Iowa;
    Texas; Illinois; Indiana.
- 3) Of Earth (mostly)   94
    Massachusetts; Rhode Island; Alabama; Wyoming; Montana;
    Utah; Alaska; Hawaii.
- 4) Of Spanish (mostly)   105
    Florida; California; Nevada; Colorado.
- 5) Of Mexican (mostly)   110
    New Mexico
- 6) Of English (mostly)   113
    New York; New Jersey; New Hampshire; Maine; Maryland;
    South and North Carolina; Pennsylvania; Georgia; Virginia and
    West Virginia.
- 7) Of French (mostly)   126
    Vermont; Louisiana
- 8) Of District and Annexation (mostly)   130
    Washington D.C.; Annexations; Puerto Rico
- 9) The Invasion (mostly)   132
- 10) What Are Your Names?   133
- 11) Of Land (Concepts)   134
    Of Land (Visions)   135
    Of Records   136
- 12) Of Prophecy to Present
- 13) Of Healing   139
    Of Healing (of the 4 Races)   141
    Henceforth   143

PART 2 – INTER-DEPENDENCE   144
- From the Declaration of Independence (mostly)
- The Ballad of Sexual Choices   147
    "How many..."   148
    Boy Friend Girl Friend
    "Let's Play Vagina..."   152
    "Let's Play Penis..."   153
    "Let's Play Metaphor..."   155
- Globally Economical Ballads   158
    The Ballad of Rates of Exchange
    The Ballad of the Sagging Economy   159
    ...of Conspicuous Consumption   160

PART 3 – CULTURAL, HISTORICAL, and ETYMOLOGICAL BALLADS
    (mostly)   162
- "Let's Play Metaphor..."
- The Ballad of Propaganda   164
- ...of Freedoms of Speech & No Speech   165
- ...of Watergate   166
- ...of the Merchants of Veneer   167

- ...of the Screen Pulpit   168
- ...of Art and Pornography   170
- ...of Technology   172
- ...of Opinions & No Opinions   173
- Vow of the Gate of Heavenly Peace on Earth ...   175

BOOK 3 – HEROES, GODS, AND MOUSAI (MUSES)   176
- "My heroes are the little birds who sing..."   177
- We Were Naked Once   179
- Introduction to the Muses   181
- The Ballad of the Muses   183
- The Nine Mousai (Muses) From Ancient Greece   185
    Kalliope   186
    Kleio   187
    Melpomene   188
    Euterpe   190
    Erato   191
    Terpsikhore   193
    Urania   194
    Thaleia   195
    Polyymnia   196
    Tenth Muse   197
    The Art of Life

BOOK 4 – HIGHER SELVES: A SAMPLING   198
- Nursery Rhymes - Two   199
    Questions to Answer
    "And a Little Child..."   200
- Of Gilgamesh   202
- For You – Tree of Life   203
- Hymns for Aten   205
    Dawn
    Mid-Morning   209
    Noon   211
    Afternoon   212
    Sundown   213
    Night-Time   215
- For the 4 Races United   216
- Singing an Epic of Peace   218
- After-Words: The End and The Beginning   220
    * * * * *

Addendum   222
- After Notes
- Endnotes   226
- Sources Consulted and Further Reading   237
- About the Author and Publications   242

INTRODUCTORY NOTES

This introduction, although a bit lengthy, gives an overview of the entire poem. The aim in giving the reader such information beforehand is to enhance one's understanding and enjoyment of the poem itself.

Although not an 'Epic' by some standards, this 'long poem' is to be read and considered as one whole poem. Many of the pieces and sections can be read as individual poems— yet the whole, as they say, is greater than the sum of its parts.

TITLE and SUBTITLE

SINGING...because song is an integral part of Life that helps to uplift our spirits and carries us through our days and nights. One of the three original Muses of ancient Greece is called Aeode or Aiode, for "Song, Chant, or Ode".

(from Greek aoide, oide)

Also...The Music of the Spheres, and Song is a Universal language.

Poetically, **EPIC** (from the Greek "epikos" from "epos" – word, song) refers to a very lengthy poem that centers on a particular culture or nation, and the journey of a hero in order to preserve and improve upon certain elements of the culture. In this poem there is no "one" hero like an Odysseus from Homer's *The Odyssey*. Rather, the hero has many faces, as Joseph Campbell would say.

One of the 'heroes' is myself for having written the poem, as well as YOURSELF and the journey you engage by reading this poem. Also, the Hero, in the collective sense, is all those who participated in the historical events mentioned in the poem, as well as numerous individuals and teachers whose words and guidance helped germinate many poems. I humbly honor and give thanks to Teachers, Friends, Muses and Spirit for the guidance that I received while writing.

This Epic also combines both epic-storytelling and epic-cataloguing.

As with songs and the oral tradition from which much epic poetry was borne, the 'sounds' this poem makes are significant as well.

FIFTH WORLD refers to a term from Hopi and Navaho(Diné) prophecies, myths, and the tales told by the Elders from generation to generation, mostly (until recently,) only by word-of-mouth. (Also, Fifth World from the Toltec; and from the Aztec's, Fifth Sun, and their Solar deity, Tonatiuh, "he who goes forth shining". Minus the sacrificial rituals of the Aztec culture, an interesting connection.) There is also an Aztec Sixth Sun of Flowers.

The Hopi refer to various phases of planetary and cultural evolution as "worlds". Some American Indian lore describes the passageway between these worlds as occurring up through a reed, and into a pool of water. Reeds are tall grasses with hollow stems, thus, one can see the symbolism and beauty of this image. One must journey upward, through a narrow reed with little visibility, while one's whole purpose is centered on reaching the destination (ascending to a higher level)—the next 'world'. This lore could be compared with Noah's journey, or even farther back to the Sumerian epic of *Gilgamesh*. Other Indian creation myths and lore describe the entrance-way between worlds as occurring through a hole in the sky (Navaho), or up a ladder or reed (Hopi and Navaho), or a tree (Zuni pueblo), and numerous others. These themes are typically categorized as "Emergence" creation myths. Creation myths and the Original-Stories, are often key guides for the ongoing evolution of peoples and their cultures.

My current understanding is that the planet Earth is now in the process of a journey from the ending of the Fourth World or Cycle (which requires 'purification')...to the Fifth World, and that this Fifth World can be seeded by one's consciousness and way of being. Many (like the Navaho) already live with this Fifth World consciousness, and each individual's path determines where they are. Whether one calls that "state of awareness" Fifth World, (or "Many Colored Earth" or "Changeable Earth", other names from the Navaho,) or by another more personally and culturally appropriate name, is rather insignificant-- the true importance being progress on one's
evolutionary and spiritual pathway.

There are Nine Worlds according to the Hopi tradition/lore, and perhaps Seven according to the Navaho.

This epic is FIFTH WORLD because it honors the traditions of many of the indigenous peoples of North America. The poem is centered geographically and historically on, what many now call, the United States of America.

This is also called a Fifth World Story-Poem because any specific culture or nation is really only a starting point for
      ONE WORLD CONSCIOUSNESS and eventual WORLD PEACE.

The aim of blending various traditions and pathways is: to transcend apparent divisions and thus experience Unity. This blending also enables one to seed various wisdoms from cultures around the world into one's own personal 'field' or 'garden'.

This poem reflects a blending of what Fifth World is to me; your experience may be similar, or rather different, or to be discovered. There are also other basic aspects of what Fifth World means, and those you'll discover as you read the introduction and poem.

This is a **STORY-POEM** because the overall flow and information of the poem has a specific pathway that unfolds much like a story (though in poetic form.) This poem is also a kind of Poetic Peace Manual.

INNER and **OUTER WORLDS**...because many of the topics, images, ideas and experiences mentioned in the poem can occur within oneself, as well as 'outside'. **PEACE** truly begins as an INNER state of being, and this ever-expanding state of consciousness makes for a more peaceful world. Whether with oneself, a small circle of friends and/or family, or with communities, or the entire world...whatever PEACE one makes, makes the world more PEACEFUL.

"Even *one* being at Peace puts the heart of God at rest. And God needs rest."

THE POEM BY 'BOOKS' and SECTIONS
SUMMARY

BOOK 1 - RADIANT ILLUMINATION– celebration of Light and its effects and blessings throughout the seasons.

BOOK 2 - TURTLE ISLAND – how we have, do, and will trod our paths, individually and collectively on this Earth, with various ballads for liberation and finding one's own clarity and peace.

BOOK 3 - HEROES, GODS, and MUSES – examples of inspiration and guidance (emphasizing the muses of ancient Greece) for living happily in the world.

BOOK 4 - Higher Selves – a sampling of illuminated examples.

The FIRST section of BOOK 1 is "THE YEAR OF RADIANT ILLUMINATION". This phrase, "Radiant Illumination", is derived from Mayan prophecies, and notes a time (Spring Equinox - March 21, 1995)[1] according to the Mayan calendar in which an "age of belief" was superceded by an "age of reason" or "real knowledge and experience". "Radiant Illumination" refers to this awakening of consciousness, and a heightened connection with the "Light".

While I do not adhere my views or lifestyle to Mayan culture, and regard their prophecy as one of many, I have adopted this phrase for its own inherent beauty, symbolism, and the signaling of an era of Awakening.

This section portrays the enjoyment and respect of, as well as devotion to...the beauty of Nature and all its co-habitants, as well as to the 'natural' awakening of consciousness so often found there.

Transcendentalists, so-called pagans (Druids), many Indian cultures (Eastern and American), Asian cultures, and your average gardener and outdoors-people often regard human beings as a tiny yet essential part of a greater whole, and thus see fit to live in harmony with the surroundings.

"AWAKENINGS" and "BLESSINGS" serve to further 'land' one's feet on the ground, and affirm a means for living peacefully with, and finding one's path within, a sometimes turbulent 'world-at-large'.

The SECOND and longest BOOK is "TURTLE ISLAND", Turtle Island being a name for the North American continent (though this poem focuses on the United States of America), as well as the Earth in numerous American Indian and worldwide 'mythologies'. This section honors, but in no way exclusively (as you will see) the American Indians, or Native Americans, as some say, (otherwise known as The Red Race) for their simply 'being here' first, as well as for their wisdoms and respect for all life...and for living, working, and learning WITH the land (which is much more than just 'land' to ANY indigenous peoples.) In American Indian as well as worldwide mythologies, the Turtle is said to carry the Earth (or continents) on its back.

While the Turtle is associated with Mother Earth, (especially for American Indians,) some Indian creation myths refer to Sky Woman or Sky Mother who 'fell' onto Turtle's back, and ancient Egyptians revered a sky-goddess, called Nut, whose 'body' was arched across the Heavens, and an earth-god called, Geb, symbolized as a Goose; they were often referred to as brother and sister. So you can see that what one calls 'masculine' or 'feminine' often depends on one's cultural vantage point.

"THE BALLAD OF TURTLE ISLAND" reads a bit slower (very Turtle-like,) as it was written to record and catalogue, in a factual, historic, poetic and sometimes humorous fashion, the true names and origins of the States, and to highlight the multi-cultural influences on what has 'uniformly' come to be known as "The United States of America"... Also, to honor the true natur(e)al spirit of freedom and courage, as well as the immense sacrifice and struggle of many that went into the creation of the States and the evolutionary freedoms of the specie that the States were intended to and have come to represent, in some instances, worldwide.

In my attempts to bear witness as an objective observer, I must say that my feelings and opinion, based on historical evidence, lean toward the side of empathy with the Red Race, whose homeland and peoples were systematically reduced, forced to relocate, and in some instances destroyed.

ALL of the many influences, regarded or ignored, are truly part of the living reality and ongoing legacy AND evolution of Turtle Island and the entire planet.

This section also aims to help make the learning and memory of history fun, as well as informative and educational, and to help distinguish what I perceive as the *'true* American Spirit' from what is broadly termed 'the American Spirit' or 'American Dream'. The *'true* American Spirit' is really only a form of Spirit's broader reality.

(Note: my apologies to any tribes or nations that I have overlooked or omitted mentioning. There are over 560 federally recognized tribes including over 200 Native village groups or tribes in Alaska. There are also 240+ NOT federally recognized. Over 30 tribes are state recognized, some of which seek federal recognition. Some maintain sovereignty with their own forms of independent government; these tribes maintain what is referred to as a "government-to-government relationship."[2] And some have *never* been recognized.

Because this is essentially a poem and not a full-fledged research/ historical text, I have striven to mention and highlight only some of the most significant and well-known tribes, along with some barely known (at least to me,) until I did the research.

It is significant to note that many tribes refer to themselves as "the people" or "the people of..." thus hinting at the true unity of all "peoples"... long before the phrase "We The People...." was declared in the "U.S. Constitution". The Indian tribal names are in stark contrast to the often glorified (and foreign) names of an individual.

Also, my apologies for leaving out any significant historical data. Some tribes lived in or traveled through many areas that we now call 'states'. In the "Turtle Island" section some are mentioned by the original areas they inhabited, and some in the 'states' they currently inhabit, though much of their lands are distinct areas from the United States.

Many tribe names have various translations— some of those mentioned are from tribal websites and literature; for some I picked the most common or most positive interpretations, as well as what the tribes call themselves, (many commonly known tribal names were names given by enemies or the ignorant.) The Indians' or Europeans' use of "Indian" pronunciations and translations often account for various spellings.

Some 'state-name categories' overlap. For example, Texas is from an American Indian word which the Spanish also used, yet this state is under the category "Air & Allies" because the name means "friend", hence "ally." I have chosen this type of grouping to pay homage to both the natural and original elements, attempting to grasp the truest origin, at least linguistically/name-wise. Some states are named after a river, but the river was named after a tribe, so the tribe sometimes gets prime recognition. Hence, the "(mostly)" appended to the categories.

I was rather ignorant when I first approached researching the origin of state-names. As I found out how many state names (over half) come from Indian tribes or words, I realized what a debt is owed to the Red

Race. And so began the impetus for "The Ballad of Turtle Island"— to record historical facts in a historical, poetic, and linguistically accurate manner, and to awaken appreciation and respect for a People who have been grossly mistreated in the past. Hopefully this poem will also help to show that the American Indian Peoples are alive and well, with some strong and flourishing while many still deserve far more equal treatment.

While 'American Indian' is commonly accepted as an overall term for such a large grouping of peoples, some also use the term 'Native American'. I prefer to use the term American Indians, as many peoples are Natives of the land yet not "Indian". I also use the term "Red Race" as a recognition of an entire people and their place among others. Some say that the term Indians came from Columbus' mistakenly thinking he reached the West Indies, or India (though that was called Hindustan then), and others say Indians comes from the phrase "In Dios" or "with God, or, God-within". Also note that "Indians" is a broad term, and though there are many, many cultural similarities, there are still over 700 distinct tribes!

Eskimo, Aleut, Inuit, Inupiaq and Yupik are not considered American Indian, (though they are certainly "native",) with the Eskimo and Aleut preferring "Alaska Native."[3] Yet there is much in common as peoples.

Mentioned throughout, though not as distinctly, is the other historically mis-treated race, the African-American. Because my 'starting point' is based on the name-origins of the states, I have highlighted the American Indians.. yet also acknowledge that the names of the United States sadly lack ANY recognition (to my knowledge) of the Black Race-- though city, town, etc. names may show some respect in that regard.

Further "BALLADS" in this section focus on topics or incidents that have shaped various attitudes and human laws, most of which deserve serious re-examination in order to encourage personal and collective liberties, or as the Declaration of Independence states: "..life, liberty, and the pursuit of happiness...", or "uncontrolled enjoyment" as William Penn expressed it.

This section portrays some topics that many people grapple with in order to make sense of the world, and thus arrive at their own open-minded choices and experiences of what 'constitutes' a free and healthy lifestyle. Some of the inspiration for this section comes from the Scottish poet Robert Burns and the theme of poems "against secular tyrannies," or, in support of human freedoms and liberation. Thus, this section has ballads on sexuality, the global economy, along with historical, cultural, and etymological topics. This section also honors the fact that one must sometimes express Anger (and preferably not violence,) in order to have Peace.

Having traveled through the states geographically and historically to the 'present,' and looked toward the future...one must then be PEACE-FULL to gain entrance/access to the THIRD BOOK in order to meet "HEROES, GODS, AND MUSES."

The topic of heroes asks us to look at who are the heroes in our daily lives and in the broader and mythical sense.

The experiences and realms of the various "MUSES" can also be applied to one's personal life—whether one is a 'typical' artist, or simply of an 'artistic nature' such as a chef, baker, athlete, etc., or simply a human being with whatever self-definition you have regarding 'the art of life'.

Finding so little else written about the Muses from ancient Greece (perhaps they prefer it that way), I found it useful to at least list them with a brief poetic description of the realms of creativity (arts and sciences) attributed to their divine origins.

As to the "personal muse" that so many artists refer to, I can only say that I experience that presence but could not be sure that the "personal muse" is not some offshoot or combination of the traditional muses. Nonetheless, a "personal muse", (whether unique, traditional, or both), has a unique gift for each of us, and THAT is certainly a gift to be treasured!

"The Muses" poems (especially those of ancient Greece) are available to assist artists of various art forms in their endeavors, in whatever way they so choose, and can be adapted or reworded for personal use (such as prayers and invocations) though what you will experience is an individual thing depending upon *your* personal journey. Certainly the Muses have been helpful to me, and the poem would perhaps never have been written without their help.

May the poems on the Muses serve to help you connect with your own form and presence of any personal and/or collective guiding Muse(s).

The FOURTH BOOK, "HIGHER SELVES", aims to express and convey a higher level of inspiration and experience...beyond conflicts... experienced when one has transcended negativity, and other forms of limitation...and allowed the 'natural flow of life' to occur...that is, when one has connected one's life with Spirit in some form! This section draws on such examples as the ancient Egyptian Aten; the Kristos; rhymes of Dr. Seuss; the worldwide Tree of Life; and the Four Races.

As this FOURTH and last section reveals, (and many world philosophies, teachings and pathways remind us,) words, though helpful in pointing a way, are essentially only guides and signposts to actual experience and personal evolution. Nonetheless, words are interwoven with experience, and they are powerful tools that help to shape our lives in various ways. The blending of words AND song is often part of the very fabric that carries us through our days and nights—ever higher toward our celestial origins.....

Well, that's the basic overview...now a few more explanations and then you shall be quite ready to begin this little journey.....

CALLIGRAPHY AND ARTWORK

The Chinese brush-calligraphy and brush-artwork are here to complement the printed word, and to serve as visual and symbolic frames of reference. Symbols and pictographs often carry more potency than any number of words. The calligraphy also honors the Asian (Gold or Yellow Race) from which many non-violent philosophies, wisdom-systems, and high arts have come. Many symbols and pictographs found on rock, shell, bone, hieroglyph, etc. (with some on tortoise shells and cattle 'oracle' bones as far back as 16th-11th c. B.C. from the Chinese 'Shang Dynasty') often give a clearer insight into the original and/or truer meaning of words, processes, and a people's cultural and spiritual practices. For example, the original Chinese pictograph (a picture representing words or ideas) for "island" is-- a "bird" resting on a "mountain". This reminds us that we are souls, able to fly anywhere, and that we also find peace and regeneration on our personal and collective little "islands".

The original Chinese pictograph for the word "to speak" combines a swinging "door" or "gate", and a "mouth", and, "to hear" combines a swinging "door/gate" and an "ear." Thus, both "to hear" and "to speak" require a kind of 'opening' and 'closing'. These kinds of interpretations give added meaning and symbolism to universal human experiences, as well as to the words we use to describe them.

(Ideographs represent a combination of pictographs to convey another word or 'idea'. For example, "to speak", combining the pictures for "door" and "mouth" could be considered an ideograph, yet I use the term pictograph to refer to the original 'pictures' used. In a few cases, I have added the modern Chinese characters so that the reader can see the variations that were made over time, mostly to allow for faster writing, and sometimes because of scribe errors or ignorance. The Sun was originally a circle with a dot in the center, but the modern form is square-shaped with a small horizontal line inside.)

In the Chinese tradition, Writing or Calligraphy (brushwork,) along with Painting (brushwork) are considered the "twin sisters". For this poem I have chosen 'written English' (my native language) and 'Chinese calligraphic brushwork' (self-taught while studying Taoism) to serve the purpose of honoring a tradition that so nicely blends 'art' (pictures) and 'words' (language), and reveals their interconnected-ness by so naming them the "twin sisters". (American Indians refer to Corn, Beans and Squash as the Three Sisters because they encourage each others' growth, and the Muses of ancient Greece are regarded as Nine Sisters.)

SEXUALITY

Another subtle theme is the acceptance of various sexual preferences. The expression of brotherly Affection and Love.... is one of the antidotes for an overly aggressive and war-torn planet. Simple affection between father and son, uncle and nephew, childhood playmates, and grown-up friends is sadly lacking as a normal form of expression of brotherhood in the world. Full-fledged acceptance of various pathways of sexuality is also lacking (though much progress has been made recently.)

Even if you find such lifestyles incompatible to yours, by respecting the the lifestyle choices of others-- you honor a lineage and culture that has helped you to be 'democratic', free, and to have an interest in reading such a work as this poem. I am referring to the culture of Ancient Greece, from which our word "democracy" as well as the specific names of the Muses, numerous philosphers, and much, much more comes from. This culture was well known for its openly gay and lesbian lifestyles and self-expression.

Although some believe that such 'love' is 'impure', a simple look at history and the world today will show where such narrow opinions and their attempts at repression have led to.

Another theme is the celebration of: the 'Femininity' of women; and holistically, as a trait or behavior within men. The experience of the Anima and Animus, as put forth by Swiss psychologist Carl Jung, reveals to us that there is a Feminine-aspect within all males, and a Masculine-aspect within all females.

THE 4 COLORS, PHASES, RACES

Another not so subtle and recurring theme of the poem is the references to BLACK, WHITE, RED and GOLD. These are the colors attributed to the four phases of both physical and mystical alchemy, in which a base or lead stone is transmuted into gold, and represents the progression of that process. Literal gold has been the reported aim of some alchemists, while for others it is a mystical 'gold' that is beyond any material gain.

With mystical alchemy, there is the Black or Nigredo phase (the unknown, chaos, massa confusa); White or Purificatio (purification); Red or Fulminato (rapid and intense growth, 'heated-ness'); and ultimately all impurities are removed or transmuted and one attains, Gold or the Magnum Opus (the Great Work, the God-self, Enlightenment). This is also represented with Jungian psychology as the 4 phases of individuation: Shadow (Black); Anima/Animus (White); Self/Hero/Ally (Red); Highest/God Self (Gold) – attaining the goal of a fully liberated self, thus enabling one to further assist the evolution of the World Soul.

Various American Indian lore, specifically a prophecy as told by Baha'i-Cherokee Lee Brown, states that the bringing together of the 4 races signals healing and unity for Humanity and the planet.[4] Thus, honoring the 4 races and bringing them together in whatever beneficent ways we can (even within oneself), certainly helps us all along the Path. Recent crises -- Kenyan floods and Chinese drought; southwest wildfires and southern/midwest floods (U.S.A.); etc. -- attest to imbalances.

The regard of these 4 Races in no way implies that one is less valuable or less honorable than any other, but that each are manifestations of the Creator, entrusted to 4 different races.. each a reflection of the One Self. With so many peoples on the planet with varying skin color and ethnic/race origin, one can look to "The Rainbow" of colors, or perhaps different phases of each of the 'four prime or symbolic' colors so as not to feel excluded. Recently, the USA has had an increase in Hispanic and Latino population, which some refer to as "Brown". This might put the Brown-skinned people closer to "Black", or possibly the "Red" depending on the frame of reference, such as heritage or skin color. All this is perhaps another field of study for another writer.

The country of India, (having the 2nd largest population on the planet, as of mid-2002), would probably be considered Black/Brown (according to a Punjabi friend that I asked.) China (1st largest) and India combined make up over 1/3 of the entire world population of approximately 6.1 billion!)[5]

Many South and Central American peoples, such as Mayan, Incan, etc. (often called Indian,) would probably be considered Red. Yet, regardless of classifications and categories, each Race, each people...has unique gifts, as well as particular struggles to overcome.

Other categories that come to mind are Olive-skinned/Mediterranean; Albinos; and perhaps even a grouping of burn victims. These classifications, as I understand them, are meant to teach us something about each people, and about our path as One People on a planet. However 'true' these classifications are, you may witness or experience for yourself.

The honoring of various people as living examples of these Four Races helps to show how each Race has contributed (and still is contributing) to the evolution of the planet (as a whole) and the U.S.A./Turtle Island (specifically). Many traditions honor these 4 (or very similar colors) in their traditional circles and ceremonies.

Perhaps these 4 'primary' or 'symbolic' races and Human colors, along with every benevolent and peaceful culture and race, (and all benevolent and peaceful people,) being who they truly are, and being respected and honored for who they truly are...would bring us all closer to, or completely living harmoniously on Earth with...the Creator!

It is interesting to note that much of the historical conquests and subsequent slavery and abuse of various peoples throughout history has been for the acquisition of gold for wealth of a strictly monetary value, and the dominance (often in the name of religion or 'progress'), that unfortunately, so often goes along with those greedy desires. And that is another reason why the 4 colors/phases/races are mentioned: so as to show some examples of where the quest for material gold and greed has 'lead' us, as compared with honoring the true wealth, purpose and beauty of all people and their quests (and achievements) for personal and collective spiritual attainment. This 'golden spiritual attainment' and the radiant steps along the way reflect a re-union with our god-selves. These god-selves DO manifest on Earth (despite what most religions say of a Heaven far removed from our 'sinful' selves.)

Though we are multi-dimensional (spiritual) beings, by living in a material world we must adapt to various physical laws. But the fixation on the material as the ONLY reality, and the worship of the material have certainly wrought much chaos on the planet.

Thus, the poems on the 4 races are meant to represent respect for alternative and healing pathways for Humanity's energies and endeavors.
Om Shanti Om...Peace

AUTHOR'S BIOGRAPHICAL NOTE

Part of my path is to honor and blend various traditions of humanity which essentially espouse the same ultimate goals: Peace, Respect, Truth, Enlightenment, Love, Friendship, and so forth. Some of the cultures and philosophies that shape my path are: Hopi, Taoism, Tibetan, ancient Egyptian, ancient Greek, and The Maitreyan Movement— though essentially I am a Kaballist or student of Kaballah (as Kaballah means "the received teaching",) an ancient Hebraic mysticism or yoga that also honors all beneficent pathways.

I have written poetry (on and off) since elementary school, earned a B.A. in English Literature (though mostly for creative writing), and have spent about 8 years attending and giving various writing workshops and readings. I also consider myself a 'recorder' of information, as much as a poet, and regard my writing as a form of expression of what is needed for the world AND as a reflection of my highest purpose.

Various traditions, and forms of Yoga ("Union with God,") teach 'connection' with one's own divinity (higher selves or aspects,) as well as living harmoniously with and caring for the land, animals, birds, fish, crawlers, insects, etc. as well as other two-legged peoples. And all of

THAT is at least *part* of the whole of anyone's higher purpose, along with honoring the uniqueness (and sameness) of our individual (and collective) journeys.

Since much attention of the poem (and deservedly so) is on the American Indian roots of much of the land now called The United States of America, I must add that I am not of American Indian heritage though I feel a strong affinity and respect for their teachings and ways. I have spent a little time visiting the Pueblos of the Southwest, and have set foot on Hopi and Navaho lands, and the Shinnecock Nation Reservation on Long Island, and have met several 'natives' of various tribal lineages and found them all to be some of the most sensitive, intuitive and loving beings I have ever met.

* * * * *

HOW TO READ THIS POEM

Try to read (at least) complete sections, or parts of sections at one reading to get the overall feeling and flow.

So as not to disrupt the 'poetic flow' and enjoyment, the "endnotes" (listed numerically#,) are primarily for reference and proper recognition purposes and do not require constant checking to understand the poem. There is also a "sources consulted and further reading" list.

HOW TO USE THIS POEM DURING and AFTER YOUR READ

As a reference and links: for state origins, historical data, inspirational people(s), movements, the muses, etc.

As a resource: for inspiration and ideas for your own personal sense of Peace; for encouraging your ability to find and further evolve your true path; for communities large and small; and for bringing together various groups with differing viewpoints in order to find common ground...and above.

FINAL NOTE BEFORE THE EPIC JOURNEY...

Of all the various traditions represented in this poem, perhaps you will feel an affinity for one in particular, or for many. Or perhaps you will be inspired to discover and further cultivate those of your choosing. Whatever the case, the respect for and blending of the wisdoms of various cultures through the ages is one way of bringing together those of us willing to transcend limitations, restrictive self-definitions, and geographical borders...while at the same time remaining true to our original (or perhaps a newly adopted) pathway...so as to arrive at a 'Place', called by the Hopi and Navaho (Diné) peoples...The Fifth World!

What this Fifth World is to you...and what you are to this Fifth World...
is truly yours to discover!
May this little epic poem inspire you and others, and serve as a
stepping-stone to further the benevolence of your life's journeys!

SINGING AN EPIC OF PEACE

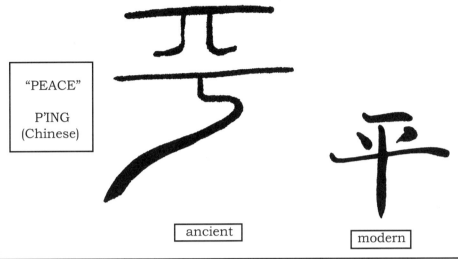

"PEACE"

P'ING
(Chinese)

ancient

modern

(ancient) The breath moves through an obstacle or shield to create peace and liberation.

The large curvy line signifies "the Breath". Above the "Obstacle" (bottom horizontal line) are two curved lines (signifying 'Opposing Forces') connected to upper horizontal line. The breath moves through the obstacle, expands Peacefully, and 'connects' the opposing forces.

This expansive Peacefulness 'rises above' all differences, brings about change, and is nourished by the breath. Breath is an action that connects all living beings. We all must breathe to live, and breath is a sign of Life and Spirit no matter what one's race or outer form.

This pictograph suggests that one's own Peace (Inner Peace,) or any form of Peace begins with the breath... a breath focused enough to move through any obstacles, transcend barriers, and thus bring about Peace by unifying, or at the very least, dispelling opposing tensions within oneself, a relationship, or a situation. Another interpretation of the (modern) refers to a Shield (protection) with Fire (flames) on either side, thus 'burning away' any 'ill-will'.

To create a more peaceful world, let us start with ourselves, and with the serenity of our very breaths.

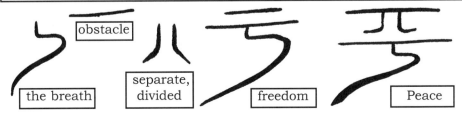

the breath | obstacle | separate, divided | freedom | Peace

PROEM: A BEFORE SONG

(Greek: prooimion pro- "before" + oime̅ "song")

Singing an Epic of Peace
Of the Deity that speaks,

From unending hidden crevices
And wide-open gathering places,
And from the central pillar
That spirals through us each—
Without cease
With devoted ease.

If I fail, sing another song—
If I succeed, sing along.

Singing an Epic of Peace
Beyond the cloak of nations and generations
Before and after the war-torn differences
Of opinions and dominions
And so, Homage To Thee Within.....

BOOK 1
RADIANT ILLUMINATION

"I want freedom, the right to self-expression,
everybody's right to beautiful, radiant things."

-- Emma Goldman

PART 1
THE YEAR OF RADIANT ILLUMINATION

SPRING

'THE PLANT-LIFE GERMINATES from the SUN's LIGHT
that REACHES even to the ROOTS'

"SPRING"

CH'UN

ancient

modern

The 'Sun' is underneath the Germination of 'Sprouts, Shoots,
Grasses, Plants'. The Sun-light gives the energy to 'crank', or
give existence to the Sprouts, etc. Hence, from the Sun's
Humble Radiant Illumination the Sprouts Emerge (above the
horizontal line — 'the earth') and grow further. Consider how
Sun-light penetrates into the ground and helps plant-life grow...

The Sun-light, having penetrated to the roots, then finds the
way upward (as a participant of plant-life) to then experience
Sun-light again.. sun-light within a new growing form,
greeting Sun-light. A kind of cellular cosmic mirroring.

This process and journey is similar to our own embodied lives
and our relating with Spirit... for we too enter a growing
'form'(the physical body) and learn to shine like the sun
toward the Sun, and play with other like-minded and light-
minded friends in the lovely Garden of Life.

PRE-FACE 1

Awhile back, you believed you had it made, had figured out the proper obeisance to the distant god.... until the spindly, green sprout shot up from the seedy ground on a day when your mind was forlorn on past loves, and broken promises, and unanswered prayers. Then, and just then, your head turned 'just so', your heart opened 'just so', your feet tickled 'just so' on the dew-drenched grass.... and that wobbly, little green sprout, barely of motion shouted silently and broke the façade of knowing too much, too little, sending you into reels of amazement, and a different kind of knowledge only gleaned from sheer experience, from simply knowing that the force from the ground is within you as well, leaving you to wonder....

why am I here?
where shall I sprout my once-bunched tendrils?
when shall I send forth for my little love affair?
how shall my green stem help to awaken another?
and though my feet remain planted to the firm,
    yet flaky ground—
who pushes my spirit air-born further and further
    from the sacred dirt?
what becomes of me now that I no longer hurt?

Now that the Spring of Radiant Illumination shines,
Now that the benevolent cleansing rain has purified,
Now that our song of peace has begun.

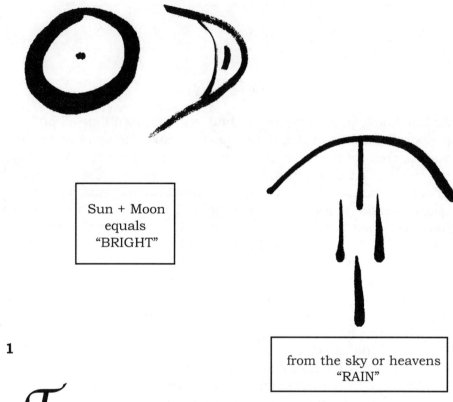

Sun + Moon
equals
"BRIGHT"

from the sky or heavens
"RAIN"

1

*T*he Spring of Radiant Illumination
that pierced through shadow—

And came a Benevolent cleansing rain...

before the frog-pond lily turned white
and Jupiter sparkled in the southern sky...
before the telepathic firefly.

The distant call of heartfelt Muses
draws near to sing through those they chooses,
and those who choose to bend an ear
can still the storm...and find inspiration here.

2

In the Spring of Radiant Illumination,
Of Luminous Consciousness,
Singing an Epic of Peace

the light grew brighter
in our dreams, and in
the full-moon mirrors

of our waking life,
and the spiral dance
was danced.

In the Spring
of long-awaited light
that led to festival night,

the light grew ten-fold in mirrored eyes
of Radiant Illumination.

The firefly's light,
the cricket's rubbing refrain...
pleasures of their own.

A pubescent cardinal
his belly redder in *one* day,

As the goldenrod blooms
like miniature suns,
the chanting of frogs

to the long, steady,
much welcome, scented rain

a cricket
awakens us to remember
a dream

WE ARE CHILDREN OF A KIND MOON
"OUT OF THE CRADLE ENDLESSLY ROCKING..."[6]

The Spring of Radiant Illumination
   That pierces through shadow...

In the Spring of Radiant Illumination
of supreme readiness,
re-surgence of energies,

sap unfurling from benevolence
of sun's illumination
and rain showering, taproot.

The slow, steady birthing
of life-liquid in trees
Winter imbedded, now shaking.

The urging motion
to *push* the tendrils,
sprout and sing.

The quiet drenched greenery,
beads of moisture
slowly, seeping in

to Spring now sounded
by common outer voices,
fanfare of birds and insects.

variations
of
"RAIN"

The dogwoods pink-white bloom
unleashes with silky reverence
and bright, light Spring.

Public display
of flesh, once winter-clothed
now itching for primal warmth.

Inner sap uncurling
to stretch and touch
the neck of a friend,

cool day,
rain-watered plants,
sex indoors

while sky, light
lengthens on the Spring blue distance...
you are near

warm, moist breath
on the earlobe,
and shape of ear

listening deeply,
to your heart-beat,

the pulse of Spring of Radiant Illumination
of Benevolent cleansing rain.

Chinese "FIELD"

The four sections
of a cultivated field.

Hopi "SHIELD" symbol
meaning
"Together with all nations
we protect both land and life,
and hold the world in balance."

3

Bright cardinal
Singing an Epic of Peace,
of numinous consciousness

what cheer-cheer trills
shakes chest and throat warmth
April's

what-cheer-cheer hear
the branches and air sound
sweet spirit

what-cheer-cheer thrills
whata-cheer-cheer-cheer
so purty-purty-purty

what-spirit thrills
shakes chest and throat warmth
April's April's

4

must be good friends,
three sparrows gathering
on a lilac branch

"THREE SMALL BIRDS ON A TREE"

Signifying 'an assembly; a meeting or gathering;
a market or fair'; as well as, literally
'a place to rest'.

The branches reach upwards, the roots...down.

5

In the Spring of Radiant Illumination,
milkweed pods
ready to burst.

A young blue jay calls
with his new found voice
"Dearest friend, and much-loved brother,
Best beloved of all companions,
Come and let us sing together
Let us now begin our converse,
Since at length we meet together,
Rarely one can meet the other...

Let us clasp our hands together,
Let us interlock our fingers,
Let us sing a cheerful measure,
Let us use our best endeavors,
While our dear ones harken to us,
And our loved ones are instructed,
While the young are standing round us,
Of the rising generation..."[7]

In these moments here together
Let us here be full and happy
Fun and full be here in earnest,

Let us do our work together
Let us play while we are working
Let us work while we are playing.

In the Spring of Radiant Illumination
That pierced through shadow,
And reached deep to soil, and soul...

Came a Benevolent cleansing rain—
Of Luminous Consciousness.

"SUN"
&
"RAIN"

from the "skies/heavens"
and "clouds"
the "rain"
falls "vertically"

SUMMER
'The GIVING HANDS of OUR HIGHER SELVES GUIDE US LEISURELY on the PATH'

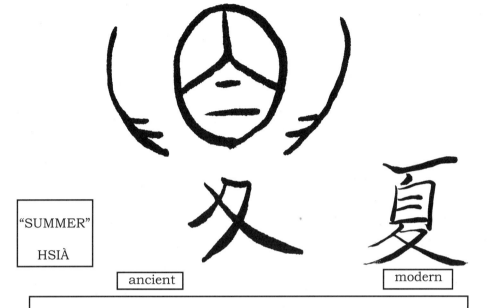

"SUMMER"

HSIÀ

ancient

modern

A 'Human Face', a 'pair of Arms and Hands', and 'a pair of Legs' with a 'line' through them to signify 'walking leisurely'.

Had the arms and hands been placed lower this pictograph would clearly resemble a person. One interpretation is that the arms and hands, because they are held downward, symbolize 'hands of GIVING'. Another is that the arms and hands are held downward and thus signify that the work is done, and plant-life will grow of its own accord during summertime.

And yet, the hands are higher up, as if coming from the heavens. Perhaps these arms and hands are like the rays of the sun, as is depicted in ancient Egypt by the sun's disk: Aten.

The hands might also represent caring for someone, as the hands embrace the face the way one would do with a close friend or loved one. Or, they portray the focusing of one's attention—a reminder to keep focused on one's path.

As well, the arms and hands could simply represent the heat of the summer sun on one's face, with the face also hinting... that we are each capable of 'Solar consciousness'.

PRE-FACE 2

Your arms reach down, and you look toward the baking sun,
reflecting on what was once your thin green wisp of a wish for
spring to find you circled with blooms and friends from all walks
of life. Your little love affair has grown, for now you have tasted
the perspiration of hard work, and the perspiration of friends who
have journeyed far just to be with you..... as you would journey
too, just to be with them, and they too would taste the knowledge
of your brow, each slaking the other's thirst—
   as the river rides to the salty sea,
   as the rain gives back what was meant to be.

Now that the Summer of Radiant Illumination shines,
Now that the work is done, for now...
Now that our song of peace has gathered friends.

6

In the Summer of Radiant Illumination

amid foggy spins
of moistured air,

came another
green morning,

lined with birch barks,
peaking light, and brown
slanted branches.

雨	rain (moisture)
ニ	skies
ⳗ	vapors

make
"CLOUDS"

7

the joy of hummingbird
iridescent
red and green,

"CLOUDS"

flashes
of Kalliope, the epic muse
upon the scene.

Frogs sing-down the rain
through aqua-blue evening sky, drunk
on honeysuckle aromas.

Twilight light, amid trees
a sylvan glow whispers
'the light emanates from circle'

8

from the light of the moon
a familiar tune
in the dream of your room

the birches first green,
the beloved once dreamed
NOW! Suddenly seen.

Let us share in deep soul-nature,
Let us love the one within us—
Singing an Epic of Peace!

9 (*a mountain in Switzerland, "young woman, or maiden")

Jungfrau*, flourish your green fields
flower-laden and cow-belled,
beneath blue-skies snowy peaked

with gushing water down
inside, through ancient rocks, inside.

The Swiss say: they can taste
the fields' flowers in the cheese,
know the locale where the cow,

cow-belled and bowed low,
savors grass and wildflowers.

The yodel and the long horn
call from town to town,
neighbor to neighbor,

a low bellow that rises,
sounds off mountain

onto meadow and ear.
This calling we must hear
gushing down

inside, through ancient gestalt,
Inside.

10

The Summer of Radiant Illumination
only the tree grows
and the fan blows
spins the warm summer air

tree grows
fan blows
whirls warm summer air

the tree grows
light green sprays
reaches for deep green days

only the tree perks
rounded with sunlight
curved with a soft breeze

reaches with steadfast ease
holding its own.

The Summer of Radiant Illumination
borne of wood and prayer
only the sitar sings
from skin-played strings

only the tree grows
and the fan blows
spins the warm summer air

tree grows
fan blows
dervish fan whirls

twirls summer warm air
and, yes, my love is fair,
my true love is fair

Only the tree grows!

"TREE"
branches go up, roots down

11

The Summer of Radiant Illumination.....
an orange moon rises, rises
Singing an Epic of Peace

AUTUMN

'The HARVEST of HUMBLE ABUNDANCE'

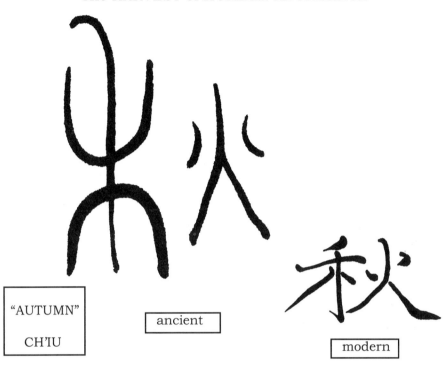

"AUTUMN"	ancient
CH'IU	modern

The 'grains, cereals or corn' ripen, or, have been ripened by the 'fiery element', and are ultimately cooked by man-made fire.

(ancient - left half) A 'Tree' with the extended and bowed middle-line, signifies 'Grains, Cereals or Corn', the long middle-line being the literal 'weight of the crop', as well as symbolizing humility and thankfulness at such abundance. 'Fire' (right half) - flame with spark on both sides, or, sticks with two flames.

An American Indian (Abenaki) myth regarding the origin of corn[8] describes a corn maiden telling man to drag her across the fire-burned ground from which a grass-like substance, akin to hair, would sprout from leaves...and eventually seeds would be ready. When the Indians see "silk" on the cornstalk, they know that the corn maiden is with them.

PRE-FACE 3

Your head is bowed with the weight of thankfulness.
Your forebears lovingly dragged themselves through field and
crowded street to put food on the table, to feed the sprouts
they had watered and watched grow, talking all the while
to the fiery sun, the cooling wind, the parched earth,
the thunderous rain, the woody root.....
praying—
     just enough, Lord, just enough so they may grow strong,
     grow up strong enough to bamboo-bend with the wind,
     tulip-open with the light,
     duck's-back with the heavy rains,
     sponge-expand with the soiled earth

     grow up just strong enough to love you for all of *that,*
     grow up just strong enough to give back to the world,
     just strong enough to pray too, so that others may unfurl

Now that the Autumn of Radiant Illumination shines,
Now that you have harvested what you planted,
Now that the song of peace has borne fruit and spread wings.

12

The Autumn of Radiant Illumination,
Into the Autumn of Radiant Illumination and long diminishing
outer light

a cool wind on the pond
reshaped education.

Aspen barks
curled up like scrolls,
above the lake
the beavers wove.

13

AH! it's Autumn ....
and the air smells good!

So remember—
Do jump carefully
in this solid dream!

14

In the Autumn of Radiant Illumination
Autumn's prism is green,

the bright, white sun
giving way, to slow tint
array of refractions

the withdrawing of sap
coupled with goose-bumped skin
giving way

to aerial migrations,
cave contemplations,
and trees stripped clean.

Cool wind! my friend,
invigorate
and crisp my steps

and breaths
along the long
trickling trail

with Autumn's prism green.

15

Singing an Epic of Peace,
Bear rolls a brown paw walk
along vein of white quartz
inlaid by mountain way.

Cinnamon fur, back hunched
near smooth rocks,
into white stalk, gold fan
aspen grove.

"MOUNTAIN"
outline of a mountain range
seen from a distance

You tell about
flute you played
to one who came
to your fire.

A guy with a ripped-up backpack
warned you,
said he warded them off
with flame from his stove.

Bear crept up.
You reached for your flute.
Notes hit the air on time.

I chew seeds, raisins.
You put teeth to apple.

We cut across rocks,
toward trail.
Listening for paw walk,
eyeing for brown one.

"FLUTE or BAMBOO PANPIPES"

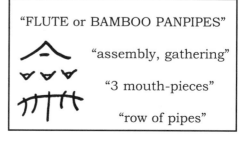

"assembly, gathering"

"3 mouth-pieces"

"row of pipes"

16

we are dumb
before the Spirit

our knees wobble
at the sight of a wren

we know nothing
but the joy of this tiny backyard
filled with birds at dusk

a rabbit and squirrel
and chipmunk

17

and a long, steady, much welcome, scented rain,
and a golden harvest
of coffee, tobacco, beans and potato,
strawberry, cranberry, tomato,
pumpkin, melon, corn, and acorn squash,
apples, onions, peas, grapes, plums, and sunflowers

out of the ground and from the trees,
out of the Autumn of Radiant Illumination,
out of the Autumn of long diminishing outer light,
out of the Autumn of Radiant Illumination and
    Humble Abundance—
Singing an Epic of Peace!

WINTER
'Even the SUN's CONTAINMENT TRANSCENDS COLDNESS'

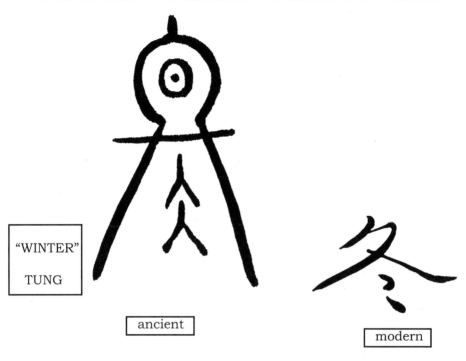

"WINTER"

TUNG

ancient

modern

A 'Loop' at the 'End of a Thread' is secured by a 'Brooch or Tie' (horizontal line); within that loop is the 'Sun', and below are 'Ice Crystals'. This 'End of a Thread' is the end of a year where the 'Sun' is contained.

Ice crystals remind us to tread carefully and the whole pictograph reminds us of the containment of winter-time, when one must 'hold with' what one has.

At Springtime, the emerging sun-light is contained again (below the roots), yet assists the germination process...
as the entire cycle begins anew;

in Summer the rays from the sun guide us;

and, in Autumn, the fire ripens our processes and forms
of nourishment, thus giving the blessings of this four-fold cycle.

The pictographs give us a clue as to the Pathway of the Seasons, as well as our own paths that encompass attuning to the world and nature throughout... The Cycle of Seasons.

PRE-FACE 4

The thinning vine and the threaded loop both remind you of the tender green sprout, the questioning and all the wondering of what will be, but the crystal snowflakes, all white, no two the same, bid you tread on foot to safe haven, when only then can you safely harken back to all the love it took to guide you home, and to put edible things in the cabinet and in the bowls, just enough to see the season through, just enough to gather 'round the fire weaving tales of then, and now, and what will be...as the blanket of snow night-covers the canvas, and no, no, the little green shoot, the once wobbly sprout is not gone beneath the frozen crust, has not withered beneath the icy snow, for yes, yes, yes, yes, yes.....
    the stems, and friends, and wind-swept bends
    have all found homes inside of you.

Now that the Winter of Radiant Illumination shines,
Now that you have faced the mirror,
Now that you have gone through the eye of the needle,
Now that our song of peace has truly received roots.

18

The Winter of Radiant Illumination...

the pond froze - -
cool, blue-white

the stoked fire sparked
and sputtered, and warmed—

"FIRE"

19

In the Winter of Radiant Illumination,
flapping geese give an aerial wave
both wing and oceanic,

Chickadee-dees December branches....
'no matter cares don't panic'

Betwixt, between
The Maker weaves
One season to another.

20

The Winter of Radiant Illumination
the Winter of long awaited return of outer light,
the slow rebirth of burnished sky

Inside,
the stoked fire sparks
and sputters and warms,

further Inside,
our wheeling lights
resemble blossoming flowers,
and star-filled sparkling nights.

21

sky worlds, snow hush,
as if the pure white sheath could
mask the active slush

as if the pure white sheath could
clear the mind of eggs & bacon
and friendship's made by blue jay's tree
where nothing is forsaken

subtle sound of boots on snow,
funny way the wind blows

22

The Winter of Radiant Illumination,
in the center
of this snow
a black squirrel

his ears tufted
toward the top of the pine
he embraces.

Our vision rises
to distance, and the squirrel
is longer there.

Around the mountains...
layers of misty snow, slotted cloud,
lean of mountainside

rolling back upon each other—
and it's all like seeing an onion
from the inside.

In the center of an onion—
there are no tears
nor one flake of snow.

The squirrel did not stay long
because this is not his storm.

Even Thuban,
the white giant in Draco,
left the center to the North Star

(after the Great Pyramid was built)
only to return someday, after Vega
has its shift again.

Echoing light of stars
and steady float of snowflakes
surround us

> there is
>   very
>   little
>   dizziness
> in
>   this
>   position

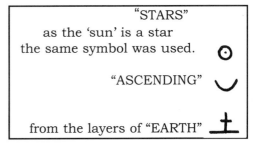

"STARS"
as the 'sun' is a star
the same symbol was used.

"ASCENDING"

from the layers of "EARTH"

29

23

In the Winter of Radiant Illumination,
Sunrise over anywhere,
through the bathroom window

branches silhouetted.
Water in the sink....
how warm the skin when wetted!

A face shows time, as well as place,
as well as deep emotions,
and Sun befriends cold winter air
as well as mirrored motions....

24

all Winter for Spring's
soft soil, moist breaths—
slowly rising....

"FLOWER"

a branch or stem (middle-line)
with leaves or flower-petals (both sides)

the breath moving through an
obstacle (see "peace" - page 1)

This suggests the mysterious growth
of flowers...nurtured by some sort of 'organic breath'.

25 - CYCLE OF SEASONS
And the Luminous Consciousness,
and the Mirrored-Eyes,
and the Spring of Radiant Illumination
with a benevolent cleansing rain,
'the Plant-Life Germinates from
the Sun's Light that reaches even to the Roots';
And the Summer of Radiant Illumination
   with peaking light,
     'the Giving Hands of our Higher Selves
     Guide us Leisurely on the Path';
And the Autumn of Radiant Illumination
   with a cool wind invigorating,
     'the Harvest of Humble Abundance';
And the Winter of Radiant Illumination
   with a stoked fire sparking and warm,
     'even the Sun's Containment
     Transcends Coldness'—
And the Whole Year of Radiant Illumination
of long awaited Light!
From sun germinating sprouts,
to the giving hands of the serene path,
to the fiery ripening,
and containment of energy,
on the path of Radiant Illumination.

Singing an Epic of Peace
Of the Deity that speaks,
From unending hidden crevices,
And wide-open gathering places,
And from the central pillar
That spirals through us each—
Without cease,
With devoted ease.

If there is failure, sing another song—
If success, sing along.

Singing an Epic of Peace
Beyond the cloak of nations and generations
Before and after the war-torn differences
Of opinions and dominions
And so, Homage to Thee Within....

PART 2
AWAKENINGS

"First Light of the SUN"

1

AND SO

six a.m.
crow caws
the sound barrier
between dream and so-called reality

And so
move gently

into the pristine
shimmer of first light
for only doubt can split the worlds apart

And so
step calmly

into day's first sight
with the sounds of crow
where tongue and mouth-roof touch

ocean's pleasant churning
near to ear

presence of beloved
within reach

And so
whole-hearted dream
within one's chest

"DAWN"
The Sun just above - the horizon
or the digit 'one'

2

Walking the Path—

Put your feet to the Earth
She loves to be touched

Put your eyes to the Sky
He loves to be seen

Laugh with the Moon.

Put your ears to the Ocean
She loves to be heard

Put your tongue to the Stream
He loves to be tasted

Dance with the Wind.

Put your nose to the Flowers
They love to be smelled

Be with your Brothers and Sisters
They Love to be Loved

And Be One

Put your eyes to the Sky
She loves to be seen

Put your feet to the Earth
He loves to be touched

And Be One

3

BROTHERS

Trace the curve
of arm and sinew

Heal the tender tension
of having withheld touch

Warm meld,
skin and fingertips,
Brothers—

of Love,
None too much.

Trace the maps
of war-torn strifes

Heal the strain of dusty holy sites,
of having withheld touch

Gentle meld,
skin and fingertips,
Brothers—

of Love,
None too much

4

SISTERS

cross-legged, conversing,
and on their knees the long day,
planting impatiens

5

SONGS: SOUND AND SILENCE

> The ancient Chinese pictograph for the verb "TO HEAR", combines a "Swinging Door" or "Gate", hence the two panels, and, an "Ear". A rather illuminating description for the act of hearing....
> teaching us that True Listening requires knowing when to Open and Close one's ears.

i
There is the song of silence
unheard between odd moments
between the notes of birds
singing the day round
into a round prayer
and carried henceforth.

There is the song of silence
unheard between the chatter of conversation
and the jeweled expression of truth,
between the uplift of laughter
and the well-pointed angry face,
between the heated hummings
of the lover's embrace.

There is the song of silence
unheard at even spans
between the thoughts—
Meditation

ii
There is the song of sounds
of cups and liquids easily poured,
the poised splashing of liquids,
the streams of running waters,
and the gentle footsteps
upon the firm and yielding earth.

There is the song of sounds,
the clicking of trees, the crackle
of bird-seeds and splash of bath-water,
the wooden gate's clattery-knocks
for no one's answer,
and the voices of the day's bidding
carried henceforth.

There is the song of sounds
of the whirr of time and space,
place to place, and the voices
uttered for millennia, and to be uttered
for millennia from the god-hearts,
god-throats, god-vocal cords, god-teeth
and god-tongues less dense,
and from the silence

Without cease
With devoted ease.

There is the song of sounds
the clicking of trees, the crackle,
of the whirr of time and space,
of bird-seeds and splash of bath-water
place to place, and the voices
the wooden gate's clattery-knocks
uttered for millennia, and to be uttered
for no one's answer,
for millennia from the god-hearts
and the voices of the day's bidding,
from the god-throats, god-vocal cords, god-teeth
carried henceforth
and god-tongues less dense
and from the silence.

PART 3
BLESSINGS

1

THERE But For the Grace of God

so humble
caring for others
there,
but for
God
there but
for God
so humble,
caring for others
there but
for God
sacred here
cherish anything
but the humble
there but for God
down to earth
open-minded
us wide-eyed
invisible
blessing
there but for
God
there
but for his
infinite
grace
he has
given us here

2
A PRAYER BETWEEN HERE and NOW

i
These letters
the inspired:
   g   e   s   t   u   r   e   s   or
         j   e   s   t   e   r   s

        of One
we can only open to.

Between these letters - -
      motions and conversations with bells
            untranslatable.

ii
These words
the bits and pieces
of   a   deeper   love.

Between these words—
      colors of moments
            that cannot be painted.

iii
These lines the ribbons trailing along a breeze of breaths:
Between these lines----
                     a thousand poems
                              that cannot be written.

                  iv

                  Travelers make their way
            holding fast to the center of the wheel.

                  And those who *must* stay
                  hold fast to the nothing
                        so all may
                  proceed smoothly

(ancient)   "CENTER"
center of the 4 quarters, or,
arrow in center of a target

modern

3

Facing a moment of –
'do I give up?'

If not for the travelers
and the tree,

and each being singing
a Song of Peace,
yet, no one person can Sing an Epic of Peace—

there must be those who sing along,
along with the birds, and blossoming lights,

and you, dear reader, singing
your Song of Peace,
until the Epic sounds, and resounds

fresh as the dawn,
as sweet and sharp
as the fresh grass mown,

the sing-song carrying me
beyond such frailties as "I",

to harmony
and love

and to you dear reader,
dear listener!

4

Lady who reads this,
who has carried our children—
have you carried enough,
except for those truly desired?

Carried so much
Our planet swells,
Carried so much
Our roads swell,
Carried so much
Our schools swell,
Carried so much
Our prisons swell.

Have you not found some orphan to Mother?
Have you not found some lonely one to Mother?
Have you not found some friend to Mother?
Have you not found some child within you to Mother?
Have you not found some Mother within you to be child to?
Have you not found some lonely sister to love?

Where are the children of tomorrow
if not also with the children of art,
of stories, children of poems and music,

the brain children
and the children already with us?
THOSE OF A KIND MOON
"Out of the cradle endlessly rocking..."

Man who reads this,
who has fathered our children—
have you not fathered enough,
except for those truly desired?

Have you not found some orphan to Father?
Have you not found some child within you to Father?
Have you not found some Father within you to be child to?
Have you not found some lonely brother to love?
Have you not found some other place for your endless seed?

How fruitful can you be?
How much can you multiply?
Have you not done the math?

Where are the children already with us?
THOSE OF A KIND MOON
"Out of the cradle endlessly rocking..."
Singing an Epic of Peace!

BOOK 2
TURTLE ISLAND

The Chinese pictograph for "ISLAND"
[upper left]
is a 'Bird' resting
on a 'Mountain' or a rock in the ocean.

As souls, we are able to fly anywhere,
yet we have chosen, for a time,
to make our homes here on Earth,
or as some say—TURTLE ISLAND.

The lower curve of the bird's body and the mountain
bear some resemblance to the modern peace sign.

TURTLE/TORTOISE
Gold (Yellow) Race [upper right] -
ancient Chinese pictograph of a tortoise

<<   Red Race -
Hawaiian sea turtle from petroglyph

<<   White Race -
turtle from a textbook

<< Black Race -
ancient Egyptian river turtle

"Easy," she said. "You got to have patience. Why, Tom—
us people will go on livin' when all them people is gone.
Why, Tom, we're the people that live. They ain't gonna
wipe us out. Why, we're the people—we go on.

"...we keep a-comin'. Don't you fret none, Tom.
A different time's comin'."

Ma Joad to her son Tom
from *The Grapes of Wrath* by John Steinbeck, 1939, (chapter 20.)

*****

"...the Laws of Nature and of Nature's God entitle them..."

from "The Declaration of Independence, 1776"

*****

"Some convenient tree will afford them a State-House,
under the branches of which, the whole colony may assemble
to deliberate on public matters."

from *Common Sense* by Thomas Paine
(Philadelphia: printed. And sold by W. and T. Bradford) 1776.

*****

Mitakuye Oyasin ("We Are All Related" or "All My Relations")

    -- Lakota Indian ceremonial refrain, greeting and prayer
       honoring the Oneness of all beings
       and all the spheres of the sacred hoop of life.

PART 1
THE BALLAD OF NATIVE AMERICA (TURTLE ISLAND)

PRE-FACE

Various Indian tribal lore says that the Turtle has 13 sections on its outer shell, and that these sections represent the 13 Moons (28-day cycle) of every year.

Although the sections of "Turtle Island" (in this poem) are somewhat arbitrary, (and don't follow any specific moon cycle) the Turtle, nonetheless, (and the number 13, actually a positive and lucky number) serves as our guide here.

Now.....THE JOURNEY SLOWS..........as you hop aboard the back of the Turtle to travel various roads of Turtle Island.

This particular journey, however, is not simply geographical, but also historical, multi-cultural, attitudinal, factual, philosophical.....well... you see....the Turtle is rather multi-faceted.

The following journey does a bit of back and forth (time-wise), a bit of here and there (on the map), a bit of cross-referencing (information-wise), and so on...yet eventually, you will have covered the 'tracks' or 'footprints' (albeit brief in Turtle or historical terms) of Turtle Island.

Because some history is not very 'pretty', you may want to 'go inside' the shell at certain times not only to 'protect' yourself but also to
contemplate 'why?' some things happened the way they did, and how YOU might improve upon or help heal such parts of history that are still having adverse effects.

At other times, you may feel the urge to stick the neck out fully, so as to survey the land and territory, face up to certain events or ideas, and even speak up about such.

However you choose to journey, remember that— although your journey, perspective and actions are unique—you also ride on the back of the Mother Earth Turtle who has journeyed for ages, carrying many, many others along with her across land and sea (bearing many shocks and attacks to her shell, swimming and moving through dangers)—yet ever journeying.....Turtle Island.

You see, Turtle Island needs all the help she can get to preserve her age-old structure and wisdom; and the happier those that ride her are, the lighter the load she bears...

> With more than a prayer
> that we not lose
> our freedoms which come to us
> from many people whose
> .....lives were – and are – devoted to such!

TURTLE ISLAND

Rides through water
and on land,
Turtle gifts of Perseverance
Here on Turtle Island.

Carries a protective shell,
four legs like four directions,
sticks Her neck out, or,
goes inside, protections.

When on land...
outruns the hare.
Deep inside...
the gifts of Prayer.

Deep inside...
the Center of one's being
Meditate Creator, or,
Universal seeing.

Rides through water
and on land,
Turtle gifts of Prayer
Here on Turtle Island.

Carries the World
upon Her back,
Balancing the steady
and the fast track.

Wise old Turtle
of Longevity,
Carries the weight
of our brevity.

Rides through water,
breathes on land,
Turtle Prayer and Perseverance
Here on Turtle Island.

Turtle came upon the worldly scene
some 200 million years ago,
must truly be a benefit...
to taking it real slow.

Found on every continent, except
frigid Antarctica,
adapts to deserts and rainforests,
mountains and rivers, etcetera.

To the underworld
if you have erred,
or, on Her back
if you have cared.

Up from the depths
of Tartaros hell,
(just a name
one can dispel)

the Turtle
lifts us on Her shell,
and so, our global stories
tell,

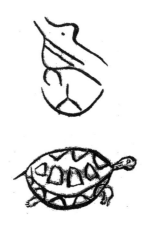

Hindu myths
and those Chinese,
American Indian
and Australian aborigines.

To the underworld
if you have erred,
or on Her back
if you have cared.

Rides through water,
breathes on land,
Turtle Prayer and Perseverance
Here on Turtle Island.

This beauteous Earth
so many call Turtle Island,
and the lesson remains—you can buy
but you cannot own land!

The Turtle
lifts us on Her shell,
and so, our global stories
tell

Hindu myths
and those Chinese,
American Indian
and Australian aborigines.

To the underworld
if you have erred,
or on Her back
if you have cared.

To the underworld through water
for a ball of earth.....
emerging again—
a worldly re-birth.

Soft clumps of dirt
upon Her hard-back shell.....
a landing pad for those
who from the sky fell.

And so, the Indian stories
tell,

This beauteous place
so many call Turtle Island,
and the lesson remains—you can try
but you cannot own land.

Rides through water,
breathes on land,
Turtle Prayer and Perseverance
Here on Turtle Island.

This beauteous Earth
so many call Turtle Island
and the lesson remains—you can buy,
but you must caretake land! ·

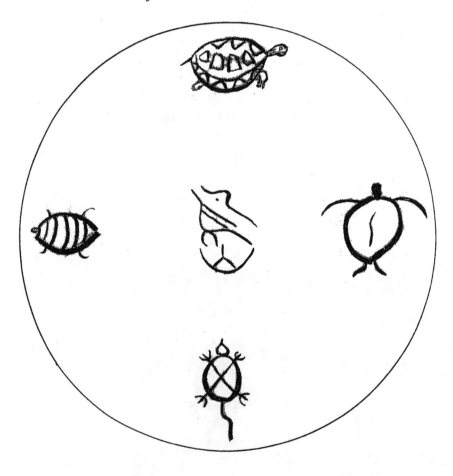

PRE-AMBLE, or, THOSE WHO WALKED BEFORE

Isn't it odd that we call North 'America'
when there's a Central, a South, and a North,
and those southerly parts were inhabited long before
the revolutionaries headed forth.

1507 for Amerigo Vespucci
for the 'new' world;
however— Amaru, a Peruvian god,
and *their* land-- *Amaruca*, from whence the U.S.-flag-name unfurled.[9]

Like the Mayan's Quetzacoatl of Central America,
Amaru "the plumed serpent",
befitting of the Ohio valley Great Serpent Mound and the Mississippian
                        temple-mound-builders and Cahokia culture
where traders from Canada to the Gulf of Mexico made a dent.[10]

Serpent mounds and carved stones of snakes
still exist on indigenous lands,
where serpent-fearing Church-goers once landed
to convert a culture they didn't understand.....

And, the names of the United States
come more from Constitutional grace
and persons of historical repute
and honoring of Indian place,

than policy would lead you know—
of patriots and independence,
and freedom from a ghastly king,
or being the supposed original tenants.

I do not scoff at revolutionaries,
nor framers of the freedom papers;
but the *neglect*—of our TRUE ancestries,
and those who are Earth's natural shapers.

The land was known—before Columbus came—
by waters and by nature's herbs
by those who honored earth, and sky, and in between—
long before the advent of suburbs.

A name serves well to honor those
who lend us light from roads they've traveled,
but blemishes on a face are made
when people from their path are unraveled.

And the names and the people
live on with grace,
first named from what
they saw or lived nearby,

of Earth
and of the flowing Waters
upon which
the people steered by.

The American Indians now live mostly on sacred, parceled lands
meted out by genocidal, warmonger generals,
who in their quest to rule the Earth
refused to distinguish—annuals from perennials!

And some tribes now are sovereign nations,
'free states' on the same kind of land, blessed;
though some confined to reservations,
proving: freedom within a police state....is freedom nonetheless.

This beauteous place—
the Red Race call Turtle Island
and the lesson remains—you can steal,
but you cannot own land!

Distinguishing the Revolutionary Spirit of America
from the 'American Dream'
is waking up to the shackles of oppression
then finding the illusion and cracking the seam.

The fiery spirit of true revolutionaries
not restricted to any governmental name,
but flowing through the earth and waters,
wind and wood to all the same.

A lineage of individuals spreading wide
their freedoms to groups and clans,
and through each pure heart embodying
the Spirit of Master Plans,

not restricted to the limits
of bureaucratic torpidity,
only limitless conduit for the clear channels
of Radiant Illuminations' lucidity.

Distinguishing the **true revolutionaries**... from the **colonists**...
from those just renaming the **imperial** bent:
is waking up to the patterns of behavior
then identifying those that are heaven-sent.

> This beauteous place
> so many call Turtle Island,
> and the lesson remains—you can take over,
> but you cannot own land!

The blending of European arts and sciences
with the American Indian natural way,
with the revolutionary spirit of accepting others
is more of the *true* American way.

Experiencing the living example
of the Indians daily way of being,
helped Benjamin Franklin (a Freemason and Rosicrucian), and others,
shape the wording and philosophy of some peoples' freeing.

The Age of Enlightenment of 18th century Europe
a wave of philosophy assisting French and American revolutions,
affecting such men as Samuel Adams, Thomas Paine;
Also James Madison, called the 'Father' of the Constitution...

though even that valuable document was skewed[11]
by favoring the wealthy, i.e. property owners,
'securing their rights', while the working-classes
were tag-lined along with freedoms on loaners.

A long-standing feud
between feudal lord
and those who steward
instead of horde

called vassal or servant
under lord's protection,
though abused by taxes and other fees--
what of One World connection?

"To cultivate", as in farmer,
is the root of 'colony'
on land to prepetuate
though colonialism's wrought with irony.

Though much has been twisted
and many enslaved,
their inspiring assembly
is forever engraved

on paper,
and electronic medium,
and in the minds and hearts
of non-violent presidium.

And the names and the people
live on with grace,
first named from what
they saw or lived nearby,

of Earth
and of the flowing Waters
upon which
the people steered by.

This beauteous place—
the Red Race call Turtle Island.
And the lesson remains—you can relocate
but you must caretake land!

1
OF WATER (mostly)

"WATER"

SHUI

< ancient >

modern

Winding through the varied lands
are natural borders called Rivers,
for transport, food, recreation and water
these veins our natural givers.

Though some forsake
and leave debris,
this most humble, most powerful of substances
rolls on, though not always quietly.

Water in our bodies,
water in our seas.
What will happen to our Waters
if we simply do as we please?

And the African-Americans, used as slaves,
when the Indians would no longer suffice,
ALL helped build the fabric of this country
with Whites and Asians and others—each one can give advice.

Respect and befriend all of the races
by at least Understanding if you don't agree,
for each of the races is a reflection of Self
and a part of the wholeness Spiritually, Mentally and Planetarily.

Conquer and befriend your Shadowy-self,
Purify the impurities of your Duality-self,
Activate the fullness of your Whole-self
Attain the perfection of your Highest-self.

(Note: The following is original poetry based on historical facts
and recorded information. Each state lists chronological order of,
and Year of - admission to the Union)

1st – 1787– DELAWARE – THE GRANDFATHERS

THEE very first state, DELAWARE,
from Delaware bay and river,
named for Sir Thomas West, Lord De La Warr:
but history adapted—is the *real* Indian giver.

Delaware Indians is the English name
for a tribe here *long* before Europeans arrival;
with dugout canoes and bark-covered long houses, LENNI LENAPE
"THE PEOPLE; Genuine, Common, Real, River PEOPLE"—
well-managed their own survival.

The Delaware river rolled through *their lands*
what are now parts of Maryland, Virginia, Washington D.C.,
Pennsylvania,Ohio, Delaware, Ontario, Indiana, Illinois, Kentucky, Iowa,
New York and New Jersey, speaking different dialects of Algonquian...
LENNI LENAPE—the Unalachtigo, Unami, and Munsee.

Unalachtigo "people near the ocean", totem turkey;
Unami "people down river", totem turtle;
Munsee "people of the stony country", totem wolf:
all have overcome many a hurdle.

How telling of the first state's name,
(a misnomer of "The People's" territory,)
attributed to a namesake 'Lord of the War'
(nothing personal, sir) and all that stealthy glory.

You could stop right here and still know the gist
of the following verses of historical rhyme,
but the names and the people and their pathways worth knowing
are listed below if you find the time.

The LENAPE now primarily in Oklahoma, Wisconsin and Canada
after 130 years of moving westward and northward again and again,
also known as "The ORIGINAL PEOPLE",
"Grandfather" and "Men of Men".

The LENAPE creation myth reportedly depicted
with etched pictographs on bark and sticks,
picked up on Earth near flowing waters—
creation ever-burning on spiritual wicks,

also currently in Kansas,
Pennsylvania, New Jersey, and Ontario,
covering a range with a warbling sound
akin to the little birds called vireo.

To numerous tribes *they* are the Elders,
worth learning of, if you bother—
for if given the chance would you not care to know
the story of your dear Grandfather?

42nd – 1889 – WASHINGTON – "THE FATHER"

Way up northwest for another 'first'
beyond the lands where 'the west was won',
<u>far</u> from the present Capitol
"You guessed it, General!"—WASHINGTON.

Yet still related to the first
he crossed the flowing Delaware,
while posing for a famous painting
on his way northwest—to retire there?

The first flag was made of hemp
but George, did you roll a spleeph?
and crunch crisp apples

"BOAT"	&	"NAVIGATOR"
rudder (top)		standing on
seat and oar		two legs

with your wooden (NO, they were hippopotamus ivory and cow) teeth!

Invented by Mason Locke Weems[12], a parson,
the 'He could not tell a lie', a form of white brainwashing,
to trick the folks not versed in history,
now *their* karmic laundry needs a Ton of Washing!

Until this day many still believe
exactly what they're told,
from those who claim to be so holy
taking land that was never sold.

I'm not saying he *did* lie, because George was a Master Freemason
versed in methodologies esoteric,
one of history's trailblazers
he cut through a lot of rhetoric.

Upon leaving the office for the very first time,
President Washington warned the People of this:
the factions and parties of governmental reigns
will attempt to divert you of bliss!

Swimming upstream the endangered salmon
an apt metaphor for transcending the tide
with prayers and festivities for the Salmon Woman
guiding the Lummi Indians and others on a longstanding ride,

far back as 11,000 years ago
harvesting fish and other edibles
from cedar dugout canoes and longhouses—
this state's roots indelible.

"CANOE"^
<"FISH"

Also gathering berries, bark and fish
near Puget Sound and Mt. Rainier,
the Nisqually (Squalli-Absch) "People of the grass country"—
found here.

20th – 1817 – MISSISSIPPI – "THE OTHER FATHER"

The other 'father' beloved by Twain,
probably Anishinabe(Chippewa/Ojibwe) known as FATHER OF WATERS
Algonquian, MESSIPI, to some "Mee-zee-see-bee",
            the mighty rollin' MISSISSIPPI
the ol', ol' man of numerous sons and daughters.

Or, Chippewa (Ojibway) MICI SIBI (SIPI) "great river",
"GATHERING-IN OF ALL THE WATERS";
where Tom Sawyer and Huck Finn befriended Jim,
and the ol', ol' man of amphibious sons and daughters.

For the Indians....canoe transportation, hunting,
fishing – the center of the universe, this mighty river;
with U.S. possession, 1803, and so-called Louisiana Purchase—
settlements, trappers, loggers, riverboat captains and millers.

The Father's head waters, Lake Itasca, Minnesota
head on down 2300+ miles to the Gulf of Mexico,
through bodies—Wisconsin, Iowa, Illinois, Missouri, Kentucky,
Tennessee, Arkansas, Mississippi, and Louisiana—from head to toe.

Backwater purifiers nourish the main stream
with tributaries to an eventual muddy mix,
down to Mississippi's Delta Blues transcending
environmental racism where chemical companies get their fix.

To quell the banks are concrete walls
though floods have displaced and millions killed;
respect for water's emotional volatility
keeps one solvent, and river tilled

with catfish farms and swimming millions[13]
feeding folks along the way.
A long, slow sunset on Father's River reminds us—
these rolling waters, the dividing line of America's day.

From 32 states and 2 Canadian provinces
roll rivers tributary,
ducks, geese, swans, wading birds, fish, otters, beavers, muskrats,
                    foxes, turtles, eagles, songbirds and plants
are fed or navigate migratory.[14]

26th – 1837 – MICHIGAN

MESIKAMI, or MICI GAMA, MISHIGAMEA, Algonquian, one of the five
"GREAT LAKE or WATER", home of auto industries MICHIGAN,
much more woodsy
before the-states-began.

Michi 'great'
and Guma 'water'
Mishigamaw:
way back when, tribes would barter.

Or "mishi-maikin-nac" 'swimming turtle'
of Mackinac Island.[15] Yet bear in mind the Lenni Lenape;
Indians first called the "BIG LAKE", Lake of the Illinois,
"the Genuine People" traveled around, you see.

"Michillimakinac", Huron for "turtle"
and Huron what the French called the Wyandot; Ontario tribes, Wendat:
"agwawendarahk" 'we are the people which live of a floating land',[16] or,
"island people", another example of those who cherish Turtle Island
                                                        a lot.

After the Wyandot (Huron) were dispersed by the Iroquois
some stayed put in Lorette, Canada;
others wandered through Wisconsin, Minnesota and upper Michigan,
then the Ohio Valley, and ultimately due to white settlement—
                    Wyandot of Kansas and Wyandot Tribe of Oklahoma.[17]

Or, the name, originally a lower peninsula
from the Chippewa/Algonquin MAJIIGAN "clearing";[18]
the state, after the lake, after the clearing named
by European explorers in the 17th century—a forestry once,

more endearing.

First the French explored and fur trade heavy
with pelts from the beaver and wolverine,
then the British took over 'til the Paris Peace Treaty of 1783.
Now mechanical beasts run wild, fed on gasoline.

Many recreation boats across the waters for pleasure
and back on shore the ample growth of blueberries.
Pontiac, a well-known Ottawa Chief, fought colonist expansion;
and from wooded groves grow tart cherries.

24th – 1821 – MISSOURI

"A River or Town or People having Large Canoes" an Algonquian term
for the Indians, then the river, then territory,
and the state: MISSOURI "CANOE HAVER" of Southern Sioux tribes
navigating waters daily, and migratory.

The Missouri(a) call themselves "Nau'tatci"[19]
(yet the river, also Algonquian, the "Great Muddy",)
and they blended among the Kansa, Osage, and Otoe,
re-assembled, and now live as Otoe-Missouria in Oklahoma ,

with their best buddy.

Historically, Missouri, Kansas and Nebraska
a veritable hotbed
of African-Americans, Anglos, and Indians:
the Black, the White, the Red.

Attempts were made to make Maine a free state,
though in Missouri, freedom to shelve,
thus keeping the 'equality'
of free and slave states, each twelve.

But the Missouri Compromise 1820-21
made Maine a free state in 1820,
and in 1821 Missouri free
to live on the land of plenty.

Then the territories: Nebraska to be free
and Kansas to be slave;
so, by repealing the Missouri Compromise
the politicians and slave owners failed to behave.

May 30th of 1854 the Kansas-Nebraska Act
on freedoms closed the door,
and planted 'bad seeds'
that would lead to the Civil War.

Yet, Hannibal, Missouri on the Mississippi river
boyhood home of "Two-Fathoms-Safe-Water" Mark Twain,
whose worldly views and honest humor
remain a voice for the sane:

he wove the three into one tale,
his first name Samuel Langhorne Clemens:
the Black, Jim; the White, Huck Finn and Sawyer;
the Red, honest Indian; he freed many from their demons,

and wrote for a San Francisco newspaper
to protest violence upon Chinese immigrants,
and although the editor refused to print:[20]
for the Gold, Twain wouldn't sit on the white picket-fence.

37th – 1867 – NEBRASKA

Shucking husks of historical NEBRASKA corn
seven main tribes appear in the grains,
Otoe, Omaha, Ponca, and (belonging to Sioux family)
Pawnee, Sioux, Cheyenne, Arapahoe—of the Plains.

"Nebrathka" an Otoe or Omaha word
"BROAD or FLAT RIVER",
the Omahas called "ibôâpka"
for the Platte river.

The Sioux, Cheyenne and Arapahoe hunted
and lived in four-legged-people-skin-tents, called "teepees";
while Omahas, Otoes, Poncas and Pawnees
raised crops, also hunted; built earth lodges and also teepees.

Between the Indians who had houses and gardens,
and those wilder hunting tribes farther west,
there were constant skirmishes
before white men arrived[21]...and you know the rest.

So it's not just the white man
to be dubbed as *the* enemy,
but the unresolved struggles between peoples
on the path to equanimity.....

16th – 1796 – TENNESSEE

Tanasi(e) the reported name for "CHEROKEE VILLAGES"
by a "RIVER" known as the little TENNESSEE;
drive along spring's honeysuckled highway
for a hint of the scents that a heaven can be.

More likely: from old Tsoyaha Yuchi Indians TANA-TSEE
'The Meeting Place', a confluence of streams,
                                "where-the-waters-bend or meet",
or Tana-tsee-dgee, "brother-waters-place" or "brother-waters"
a gathering of aquatic tribal feet.

Tsoyaha Yuchi "Children of the Sun from faraway" (Yuchi-"faraway")[22]
(now honored by the town, Euchee, Tennessee,)
of the mound builders, an offshoot of Mayan culture,
though almost forgotten historically.

Name is memory
and amnesia to forget,
and these names recorded
when many peoples first met.

Name is memory
and amnesia to forget,
and names forgotten
become historical debt.

The Creek were in areas now called Georgia,
Alabama, Louisiana, Florida and Tennessee;
the Cherokee: North and South Carolina, Kentucky,
Virginia, Georgia, Alabama, and Tennessee.

Chickasaw also in Mississippi and Tennessee;
the Shawnee in the eastern land,
Yuchi in South Carolina, Virginia, Georgia and Florida:
though together they did not all band.

The Cherokee Nation formed in 1948
and the Five Civilized Tribes (see Oklahoma) on spirit nourish:
Cherokee, Chickasaw, Choctaw, Creek (Muscogee), and
Seminole now in Oklahoma flourish!

He throbbed the hearts of many
with pelvis movements once risqué,
and sang for his twin-brother in heaven,
Cherokee, Elvis Aaron Presley, of Graceland—Memphis, Tennessee.

17th – 1803 – OHIO

Along another "FINE, LARGE, or BEAUTIFUL RIVER"
the Lenape, Shawnee and Wyandot (from the Iroquois OHEO or OHIO;)
an industrialized hub and the hot dog were born—
but four Kent State students slain, a day before Cinco de Mayo.

In America's heartland of autos and steel,
chemicals, building materials and machine tools,
rubber products, fan belts, the eastern end of corn and meat belts,
the demonstrators, "bums" to Nixon, were no fools.

They were protesting the bombing of Cambodia,
escalation of the Vietnam War,
when the National Guard came in and fired, (May 4, 1970)
"Please, someone tell me what all this fighting is for?"

OHIO, Cinco de Mayo,
sounds like just a rhyme;
but discover, perhaps uncover
a particular quirk of time.

The Battle de Puebla was the victory
of a miniscule Mexican Army over the French,
and though the Army eventually lost--
for Mexicans, Chicanos, Latin Americans—a symbolic monkey wrench.

But Napoleon III sent a ton of more troops
so the wrench only chipped the gears,
but even one small victory is a model
for courage overcoming fears.

So, Cinco de Mayo celebrates
Mexican unity,
and honors the Mestizo and Zapotec Indians
who had to fight for immunity.[23]

A cultural celebration
of Mexicans put to the test,
is certainly a far cry
from the ports and plains of the Midwest,

but it is a calendar's notation
of four students killed at Kent State—
protesting a path of destruction,
and attempts to exterminate.

...And a thousand miles off the African coast (in the south Atlantic)
on May 5th, 1821,
Napoleon Bonaparte I, of a stomach ulcer...
sailed into the sun.

Viva la Mexicanos; Vive la French;
"Live long and prosper"24 free of the despotic Brit.
Let Kent State be a warning for the American people:
revolution happens—and so it is writ.

And although he was "not a crook,"
Nixon (and LBJ) helped end the official U.S. 'policy of termination',
(from Hoover, 1949,) which sought, (and did) to terminate tribes,
and force people to assimilate to a foreign (U.S.) nation.

Formerly of the valleys, "shaawanooki",
'people of the south' Shawnee,
with Tecumseh, their leader for forty years
warding off U.S. attackers, and uniting brothers and sisters
                    with a pan-Indian philosophy— including the Lenape.

15th – 1792 – KENTUCKY
Shawnee meadows are "M'shish-kee'-we-kut-uk-ah",
and their word for Kentucky is "head of a river".
If the waters overflowed and contributed to meadows,
(like beaver-dam lakes after they dry)—
                    then water is the first-giver.

A branch of the Ohio river, is the "Little Cuttawa" or
"Kaintuckee" "Kantucqui" leading to Eskippakithiki, a Shawnee village
visited by other tribes, French, English, and Daniel Boone—
overall, a lot of trading and a bit of bitter pillage.

KENTUCKY, from the Iroquois KEN-TAH-TE
the "Land of Tomorrow" or KEN-TA-KE "MEADOW LAND",
with beautiful rollin' blue grass hills,
here, sweet horses roam...far from sand.

Mohawk(Iroquois), "kenta" 'level' & "tuckee" 'meadowland', "Ken-ta-ki".
And "blue-like place" from the salt deposits,
Mohawk for meadows: Ye-e-an-ty-yk-ta —
and the name from blue-grass place, I posits.

The little Cuttawa from the Catawba "river people"[25]
on a land of prairies and fields
where corn, tobacco and hemp,
were some of the most popular yields.

"The place of many fields" or "Prairie"
Iroquois "Ken-ta-ke", a.k.a. "Indian Old Corn Field";[26]
Wyandot "Ya, Yan, Quagh, Ke":[27]
whatever the name – a place for fertile yield

for the Wyandot (also of Kansas and Oklahoma)
on the central plains of the land. Also known for bourbon
and a Frontier man, one of many,
who sought for the west to be won.

"Cane and Turkey Lands"[28]
"Cane Turkey", explored and 'settled' by Daniel Boone,
Natural Man, Pioneer, (though he battled with Indians)
only later promoted like a colonizer cartoon.

He opened the Wilderness Road to Kentucky
like a highway through a small town
despite the Appalachian Proclamation Line
that attempted to keep the numbers of intruders down.

An American spirit allegedly instilled
in Kentucky where Bourbon Whiskey was born,
made from natural waters and mixed
with a base from native Indian corn.

5th – 1788 –CONNECTICUT
"BESIDE THE LONG TIDAL RIVER" of Mohican and Algonquian descent
the "LONG RIVER PLACE" QUINNEHTUKQUT,
yet more well known for insurance, Yale,
Mark Twain's Yankee home, and good etiquette.

QOUNEHTACUT, QUENTICUT, QUINNITUKG-UT,
the "LONG ESTUARY" of transportation
spawned agriculture and commerce in New England,
the Long Island Sound, and Industrial Revolution.

On this fertile plain, the steamboat invented
and also the first submarine.
Once a haven for fields of onions...
now they are rarely seen.

The Niantic (Nehantic) "point of land",
one people... until they split--
Eastern Niantic with Narragansett in Rhode Island
Western Niantic with Pequot in Connecticut.

After the 1637 Pequot War,
the Pawcatuck Pequot lived with the Narragansetts,
Mashantucket Pequot with Uncas and Mohegans—eventually
legalized gaming helped the Pequots recover from previous false-debts.[29]

Trade agreements with the Dutch, and English colonists,
but trouble when the Puritans came,
some Indians sided with Dutch, some English—
fur trade rivalries and wars to blame.[30]

Mohegan (Mohiksinug) "wolf people",
(from Lenape ancestors of Wolf, Turkey and Turtle clans,)
honor the thirteen sections on the turtle's back
and the pathway of moons, and Grandfather Turtle's plans.[31]

32nd – 1858 – MINNESOTA
In water the reflections of Father Sky,
many mansions and mirrors in His house:
with rain and sun he fertilizes
Mother Earth as cosmic spouse.

MINNESOTA from Dakota Sioux
     "CLOUDY, WHITE or SKY-TINTED WATERS"
from the river, and ten-thousand lakes,
"mnishota"; or "menesota",
home to Governor Jesse Ventura, and many who love ice skates.

"CLOUD"

Santee Sioux chief, Little Crow (Tayoyateduta-"His Red Nation")
with a treaty ceded most of "the peoples' " lands,
but payments delayed, and though reluctant, battle ensued,
so he retreated, then returned, and while picking berries—
                    was killed at a settler's hands.

Those 1850 to early 1860s events, a precursor to corporate scandals
where the ones to get payment are often denied,
and though the Santee traveled to Washington,
bottom line is—the government lied.

Numerous treaties between Dakota, Chippewa(Ojibwe), & U.S.
in regions of Minnesota, Michigan and Wisconsin supposedly drawn
with peace,
yet actually— restrict, then divide and conquer strategy.
To the indigenous psychology—no landlords, and no lease.

Nelson Act of 1899, the acquiring of land to sell to settlers,
but for the Indians concentration camp reservations and dispersion;
akin to the Dawes Allotment Act of 1833,
'legal' forms of territorial coercion.[32]

The state reflecting the ebb and flow:
"Watapan Menesota" 'river of turbid water',
"Minnay Sotor" 'turbid water';
"Wate-paw-mene'-Sauta" 'clear-water-river'.[33]
A shame to be considered on your home land a loiterer.

30th – 1848 – WISCONSIN
Ho-Chunk (Winnebago) or Chippewa
"Meskousing" 'where the waters gather';
Ojibwa "Wees-kon-san" 'gathering of the waters';
Algonquian 'long river', or if you'd rather

an Indian name mis-spelled by early chroniclers French
"Mesconsing", "Quisconsin"
probably "GRASSY PLACE" MISKONSIN from the Chippewa;
Congress made it WISCONSIN.

Also another Chippewa word
"Wishkonsing" "Place of the Beaver" or "Muskrat Hole";
also attributed to the French, Menominee, Ojibwa, Potawatami,
Sauk-and-Fox, and Winnebago languages,
with various spellings told:

Mishkonsing, Ouisconsing, Owisconsing,
Quisconsing, Wiskonsin, to name a few,
upon whose "grassy place"
sunlit....sparkles the morning dew.

Like Kentucky's meadowland from the river,
this grassy place with animal holes,
where legend has it a great serpent's movements[34]
shaped canyons and grooves where the water rolls.

Lots of grass for the cows
for the dairy farms, for the milk, for the cheese for the butter;
much machinery, and a lotta paper.
Lots o' lakes if you have a rudder.

Lots of Germans since the mid-19th century;
lots of white pine trees turned to lumber
which led to more railroads, more cities, more immigrants
though for progress the pine forest dwindled in number.[35]

Of the Green Bay area, Ho-Chunk Sovereign Nation
   ("THE PEOPLE of the Big Voice and Sacred Language")
the Winnebago, have been given the runaround
through Iowa, Minnesota, South Dakota, Nebraska and Illinois
                    by tribes, settlers, and government.
Now safe in Nebraska; and on Wisconsin *re-purchased* home ground.[36]

33rd – 1859 – OREGON
"From where the sun now stands, I will fight no more forever,"
said Chief Joseph from the peace-loving Nez Perce tribe
reduced, by government-backed military forces,
after gold discovered, and miners invaded...the treaties turned to jive.

Chief Joseph, (Inmuttooyahlatlat or Heinmot Tooyalaket -
   "Thunder coming up over the land from the water") voiced for all men:
"Let me be free to travel, free to stop, free to work,
free to trade where I choose, free to talk and think and act for myself."
May the gentle serve as a haven, until there are no more beserk.

Most of Oregon, Washington, Montana, Idaho and Wyoming
were carved from OREGON countries,
perhaps from Algonquian "wauregan" 'beautiful water'
where many a beaver builds with twigs and sundries.

Since there's a Connecticut town called Wauregan,
I lean toward the definition of "beautiful water",
as the name may have traveled like Wyoming
across wide-open country.... transcending borders.

Or, Shoshone word "Ogwa peon"[37]
'river of the west',
sounds Spanish though, like "agua"—
as good as mine, your guess.

Or, French-Canadian "ouragan"
for a hurricane or storm,
the Columbia river once called "river of storms"
by fur traders who kept people warm.

Or, for the "big-ear" of Indian tribesmen
from the Spanish word "orejon",[38]
but many Indians, like much of the timber....
gone.

Or, from the writings of Maj. Robert Rogers an English army officer,
first used by Jonathan Carver in 1778 on a cross-country stint.
Or, from the Wisconsin river (on a 1715 French map,) "Ouisconsink"
(Wisconsin) mis-spelled to "Ourigan" from "Ouaricon-sint". [39]

Or, "Ourigan" a Cree Indian pronunciation
of "ooligan" a small fish whose fish-oil
was abundant on trade routes and considered a medicine—
which one is Oregon? It's your call.[40]

In the eastern part of the state
wild sage grows abundant and strong,
from the Spanish word "orégano"[41]—
what is the origin of the true Oregon?....

where the Klamath tribe was 'terminated'
and then restored,
now seeking to reclaim their true lands[42]
from those who hoard.

43rd – 1890 – IDAHO
"Ee Dah How" Shoshone?
Some say that's just a made-up word that caught on,
meaning "gem or light of the mountains" or "good morning"
like a mountain whose peaks the sun rises upon.

Or, possibly what the Kiowa-Apache
called the Comanche —"Idahi",
though Comanche call themselves "our people",
"Nemene"—with spellings variously.[43]

For the Salmon River Tribe, "ida" is 'salmon'
and "ho" is 'tribe', "Salmon Eaters".[44]
IDAHO's Salmon, Snake and Clearwater rivers
once nourished MANY Indian river-feeders.

Salmon spawn in August,
roots are picked in May,
cow elk, water, storytelling,
and the sacred Dreaming Way.

They traveled across Oregon,
Washington and Idaho,
the "pierced nose" people, a misinterpretation—
the Nez Perce Indians you may know.

Nimi'ipuu, they call themselves, "Real People",
"We the People" now of north central Idaho,
WE THE PEOPLE, (not just Constitutional words)
a phrase as simple and firm as the potato.

They had a war chief,
AND (like the Cherokee, Iroquois and others) a peace chief, too;
now there's a good model
for the red, white and blue![45]

Another tribe the Coeur d'Alene (original homeland for 1000+ years.....
                    north Idaho, east Washington and west Montana)
from French, for their trading skills "heart of the awl",
though in their own (ancient) tongue "Schitsu' umsh"
"Those Who Are Found Here, The Discovered People" they are called.[46]

And Spokanes, Kootenai, Kalispell,
Colville confederated tribes,
Kootenai-Salish "we the people", (British called them 'flatheads')—
around Montana, Washington, Oregon even Canada—for many lives.

Tribal trade routes now concrete
as Interstate highways,
hold the memory of friendly barter
traveling through that maze.

IDAHO first in silver production,
with lead, zinc, copper, and gold—
but the real gems of the mountains
are the white pine trees, the people, and their stories told!

48th – 1912 – ARIZONA

Spanish from Aztec, "arizuma"—'silver bearing'.
Or, Tohono O'odham Indian "Aleh zon(e)" and Pima Indian ARIZONAC,
                    or, AL(I) SHON(AK) 'LITTLE SPRING-PLACE',[47]
an Arid-Zone of mountains, desert, saguaro cactus,
with Apache; Navaho. Hopi Nation equals People of Peace!

Tohono O'odham "desert people",
have a native word "papah" 'beans',

hence, Papah-ootam, Papago "bean people" of the Pima branch—
once corn, cotton and beans, now mostly cattle supply their means.[48]

Pima, A'-a`tam "the people", A'-a`tam a'kimult "river people"—
Creation myth: Earth formed by Earth Doctor.
They came under U.S. jurisdiction in 1848
after the Mexican War.

And, "Real de Arissona" reported to the Spanish,[49]
of the Pimeria Alta mountains 'town of silver mines',
then the Mexican, and U.S. followed
the many native signs.

Or, from a Basque word "the good oak tree",
"haritz" (oak tree), "on" (good), "onac" plural, thus "a grove of oak trees"-
haritz-onac[50], quite similar to Pima "Arizonac"...perhaps all in all,
'a mining camp with a little spring-place by a grove of oak trees'.

From the Navaho (Diné), "(we) the People",
a rite of songs and prayers called the Blessing Way,
a gift, a path, a ritual
for accepting and blessing everyday.

The healing of sandpaintings,
from Monument Valley's colored sands,
akin to Tibetan mandalas—
sand swept away... after prayers made with hands.

The healing from the sand-paintings
"place where the gods come and go";[51]
these acts of healing engineered
by Medicine Men of the Navaho.

plant
growth
from the
earth, or,
to give
birth to

Akin to the Cherokee Trail of Tears,
more than 8,000 Navahos forced on a "Long Walk"
by Kit Carson & U.S. Army, 1863– 64:
isn't it time we all had a Long Talk?

Yet taking responsibility for their own actions,[52]
(a lesson which all can abide,)
the Navaho cite disrespect of nature's laws,
    and disharmony within their own people
as leading to the "Long Walk" where some of them sadly died.

Though not condoning cruel actions
the above is an example of the futility of blame,
and, not always pointing a finger
without also looking within your own frame.

Jicarilla Apache, probably 'Apachu', for 'enemy' of the Zuni tribe,
or Awa'tehe, name given by the Ute.
To themselves Tinde, Inde or Diné "The People".
To understand a people, look to their root.

The Hopi and Dineh (Earth-Surface People)
from whence the term Fifth World:
up through a reed to a tranquil watering hole...
one of the ways their creation myths unfurl.

Brethren of the Tibetan people
at opposite ends of this One World size —
Hopi word for sunrise is Tibetan for sunset;
and Hopi sunset, Tibetan sunrise.

(1950s—one million Tibetan peoples killed,
one-sixth of population!
and driven from *their* homelands
by the militaristic Chinese nation.)

The hearing of each cerebral hemisphere
we call a temporal lobe.
And a Grand Canyon known
all across the globe.

The mysterious Anasazi abruptly disappeared around 1200? A.D.
(was it drought, or mis-guided magic, or signs from the sky?)
leaving cliff-dwellings, ritual sites,
and us to wonder why.

Yet "ancestral enemies" of the Navaho
not their true name but given by foe;
rather Hisatsinom, "ancestral Hopi",
"The Ones Who Came Before", "the Old Ones", or, "People of Long Ago".

who built pueblos,
and city-like structures in Colorado,
Utah
and New Mexico.

Currently the Hopi lands geographically inside the Navaho Nation
and for the most part they peacefully co-exist,
and though pitted against each other by coal hungry companies, etc.
these hearty peoples subsist!

This beauteous place—
the Red Race call Turtle Island.
And the lesson remains—you can buy
but you must caretake land!

And the names and the people
live on with grace,
first named from what
they saw or lived nearby,

of earth
and of the flowing waters
upon which
the people steered by.

Rides through water
and on land,
Turtle gifts of Prayer
Here on Turtle Island.

To the underworld
if you have erred,
or, on Her back
if you have cared.

To the underworld through water
for a ball of earth.....
emerging again—
a worldly re-birth.

Carries a protective shell,
four legs like four directions,
sticks Her neck out, or,
goes inside, protections.

This beauteous place
so many call Turtle Island,
and the lesson remains—you can buy,
but you cannot own land!

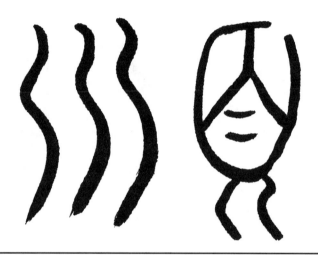

One might think that 'going with the flow' is a modern phrase, yet this ancient Chinese pictograph means just that. The 'River or water currents', and a 'Person with Legs' - 'surveying' the scene.

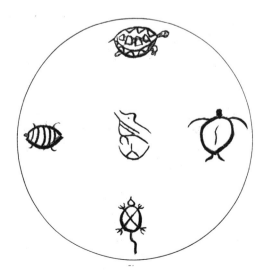

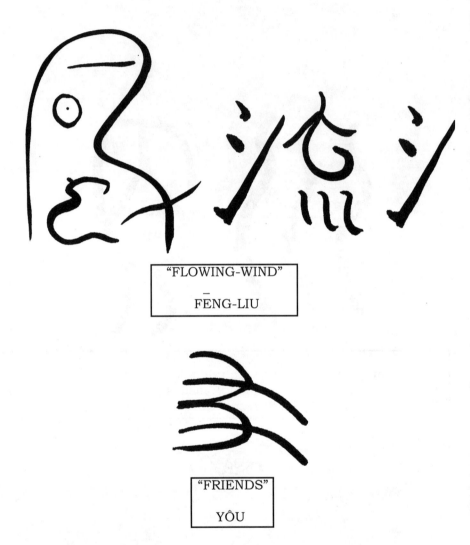

"FLOWING-WIND"

FĒNG-LIU

"FRIENDS"

YÔU

The [top] pictograph is somewhat complex, but well worth the understanding.

FĒNG-LIU
The left-half (before checkmark with two dots) is FĒNG "Wind" and is made up of five components. The largest brush-stroke signifies "extension", "expansiveness". The small horizontal-line represents the "original unity of all beings". The circle is the "sun".

The curvy brush-stroke (below the sun) represents "insects" (as they were said to be born of the "wind".) And the last slightly-wavy line (extending outside of the large enclosing curvy-line) signifies "motion".

This gives us a greater understanding of the mysterious unseen "wind". The wind goes anywhere (extends); is a universal, coming from the 'primal oneness'; is affected by 'solar winds' (a modern scientific term) revealing how much the 'ancients' knew; gives 'birth' to insects (they have their purposes as well;) and is full of 'motion'.

(FĒNG SHUI, the Chinese "art of placement", utilizes the five Chinese elements, yet is derived from FENG "Wind" and SHUI "Water". The balance of energy-flow (Ch'i) via FENG SHUI helps to create harmony and happiness with environments and personal spaces.)

The right-half [top] LIU, and "Flowing" is the simple definition, though "flowing" has a deeper meaning, and is closer to "natural" or the 'true nature of' as with the 'flowing of water'. The center portion signifies the "birth of a child", and the three wavy-strokes are "hairs", as of a "new born". On either side is "water" (probably droplets.)

Thus, this right-half of the total pictograph is an apt description of a "new-born", as well as an apt symbol for LIU "Flowing", or "the natural flow of birth and new movement".

The two pictographs together are: "Flowing-Wind", combining elementally—wind, sun, and moisture; connecting us with "original unity"; "motion"; and "giving birth".

Can you feel this effect? For the Flowing-Wind with accompanying elements give a kind of 'birth' to us, upon which we can feel our little hairs tingling, or, our entire being moving with the 'current moment'. (Also loosely translates as: 'Wind Water Flowing Naturally', or, 'Natural Child of Wind and Water'.)

&

[bottom]
YŌU "Friends or Allies" -
two hands working together, in same direction.

81

Unseen, unheard of its own nature
on water ripples, on tree and leaf bends,
barely perceptible erosion on rock face and metal structures—
this breath of Spirit befriends.

Not tasted, nor touched, nor seen, nor heard,
nor of air anything smelled,
except *that* put upon wind's wings—
yet so powerful, house and tree wind has felled.

On air most readily
our moods and currents sail,
and *that* breathed, or dust kicked up,
most easily across our globe hails.

And the African-Americans, used as slaves,
when the Indians would no longer suffice,
ALL helped build the fabric of this country
with Whites and Asians and others—each one can give advice.

Respect and befriend all of the races
by at least Understanding if you don't agree,
for each of the races is a reflection of Self
and a part of the wholeness Spiritually, Mentally and Planetarily.

Conquer and befriend your Shadowy-self,
Purify the impurities of your Duality-self,
Activate the fullness of your Whole-self
Attain the perfection of your Highest-self.

34ᵗʰ – 1861 – KANSAS

"People of the South Wind" Koln-Za,
Konza the French phoneticized Kansa,
the English to KANSAS or Kaw;
standing in the breeze you can know the real answer.

From the Mississippi river....
the Kaw, Osage, Ponca, Omaha "upstream people".
From the Mississippi river....
the Quapaws "downstream people".

Omaha (Umonhon "Upstream People")
  and Ponca up the Missouri river
(and mouth of the Kansas river)
  from the river, Akansea or Arkansas;
Quapaw, Osage, Kansa
"down" the river Arkansas.

KAW, an abbreviation of AK'A,
(first written by French traders,)
meaning SOUTH WIND in Siouan dialects.[53]
The wind guides people—even when there are invaders.

1825 to the mid 1840s
(the Indian Removal Act inclusive,)
brought other tribes onto Kaw territory—
Allotment Act psychology & 'forced suburbia'—obtrusive.

In 1872 a federal act passed,
(though opposed by Chief Allegwaho and his people,
for the relocation to Oklahoma
of The Wind People.[54]

KANSAS breadbasket of wheat,
with cows and timeless hours—
along long flat roads exclamation pointed
with silos and sunflowers!

Bringing winter wheat to Kansas in the 1870s:
were they pacifists or cowards, I do not know,
but Russian born Germans avoiding military service
gave the west another wheat to grow.[55]

Near Lebanon, KS a marker sits
at the exact geographical center
of the contiguous U.S. states. You can buy land...
but in God's eyes you're just a renter!

At the U.S. Penitentiary in Fort Leavenworth since 1976
an American Indian, federal scapegoat,
(Chippewa(Ojibway) and Sioux), Leonard Peltier, currently jailed for a
   crime he says he did not commit, (and for which there is insufficient
   evidence, and to which the government did not prove
   and admitted they did not know who killed the F.B.I. agents
   on the Pine Ridge Reservation)
of this *please* make a note![56]

The state motto "ad astra per aspera"
'to the stars by difficult ways'
and though we travel astrally—
the land we must negotiate by days.

The SOUTH WIND PEOPLE, KaNze,
one of two for movin' air,
yet ONE of many who
cherish smoke as prayer. ....

25th – 1836 – ARKANSAS

To the French, Illinois and others: Akansea,
really the Quapaw (Ogahpah or Ugakhpa) "DOWNSTREAM PEOPLE"
originally lived east; went west,
but they still had the same hull.

Downstream via the rivers Ohio
and Mississippi, to what is now Arkansas
but "People of the SOUTH WIND"
is what others saw.

Along with the Kansa and Osage
down the Akansea;
while the Omaha and Ponca
up the Missouri.

Acansa, Akensa, Akansas "People of the SOUTH WIND"
the way the air and water were flowing,
really Quapaw (O-Gah-Pah or Ugakhpa) "DOWNSTREAM PEOPLE"
by choice and necessity, must have loved their rowing.

One anchor to this streamy state
and in the dirt imbedded,
are quartz crystals which when polished clean
assist one's life unfettered.

Are-KAN-sas or ARK-an-saw
two different pronunciations,
people stress the ARK...
to be part of the nation.

Two states akin
by name, and water, and wind,
ARKANSAS and KANSAS sound different
but the people were connected to begin.

46th – 1907 - OKLAHOMA
Ani-Yi(u)n´wiya, or Tsalagihi Ayili "REAL PEOPLE"(1)
the matrilineal Cherokee Nation survived the years,
from one of the worst *forced* 're-locations'...
known as The Trail of Tears.

The Cherokee, to themselves, Kituhwa or Keetoowah,
the people "kit-Yowah" 'from God',[57]
from the name of the Creator "Yowah". Like
Hebrew "Yahweh"? Rastafarian "Jah-weh"?— we're all from One pod.

OKLAHOMA with Choctaw Nation(2),
one of Civilized Tribes Five:
from Choctaw, OKLA "PEOPLE" and HUMMA or HOMMA "RED"
plus the other (3,4,5) Nations—
                    Chickasaw, Creek (Muskogee,) Seminole—all alive!

From the Carolinas, Kentucky, Virginia, Tennessee, Georgia and
    Alabama-- the Cherokee;
from Florida-- the Seminole; from Georgia, Alabama... -- the Creeks;
from Alabama and Mississippi: the Choctaws;
from Mississippi and Tennessee: the Chickasaws[58]—
                    through valleys and peaks.

Wathohuck "Bright Path", an enrolled Sauk and Fox,
part Potawatomi, Kickapoo, Menominee,
                    born in Shawnee, Oklahoma, 1888,
known as James (Jim) Frances Thorpe;
of ALL athletes—some say none as great.

A Choctaw Reverend Allen Wright,
suggested the name with respect for the Red Race.[59]
1803 sold to U.S. as part of Louisiana Purchase;
1890 fed. government created Territory of Oklahoma, and the place

spawned outlaws and rodeos,
railroads and gold-hunts where once stood
ancient campfires and eating utensils:
1907 Oklahoma Territory and Indian Territory became one statehood.[60]

Following Jefferson's thinking, President Andrew Jackson[61]
in 1830 signed the Indian Removal Act,
(passed by one vote) forcing what he called "the savages"
to step across the track.

Starting around 1838— at gunpoint and in shackles,
from children to the old,
herded (by U.S. state militia) across a rough, wintry terrain
(at least 4000 died)—
but the spirits (of the dead and surviving) were not sold!

To honor Jackson's foregoing tillage of the soil
and instead going straight for the till,
his mug now disgraces ATM's most popular—
the twenty-dollar bill!

From tragedy to triumph
all 5 Nations live today,
OKLAHOMA "RED PEOPLE"
Unity of the Five Tribes...natural way!

And before them a wealth of other tribes,
though at some points driving out each other;
and before THAT--cave dwellers, mound builders
and Earth-House People[62]
considered the original sisters and brothers.

Then, Caddo and Wichita,
then Osage and Quapaw, and Ute, Comanche,
Kiowa, Lenape, Shawnee, Kickapoo, Kaw, Pawnee and Seneca-Cayuga—
many forced to Oklahoma, like the wailing of a banshee.

And Tonkawa "staying together"
really, Titskan-Watich "indigenous men",
Texas, Oklahoma and New Mexico the lands
where they generated....way back when.[63]

Andrew Jackson forced removal of many tribes
from the south in order to capture cotton and gold,
and in Oklahoma, after the true caretakers of the lands
were dispersed—
the infamous depression of the dust bowl.[64]

Once— they were free to roam the Plains
hunting the sacred buffalo,
then, they were penned like cattle
....yet ever on a path with sky above and earth below.

39th and 40th – 1899 – NORTH and SOUTH DAKOTA

DAKOTA "ALLIES or CONFEDERATES", three main groupings
of Dakota Sioux, of the Plains Indians Nadoussioux:
Dakota (or Santee), Nakota (or Yankton),
Lak(h)ota (or Teton)—all in all a mighty crew.

In the 17th c. the Chippewa (Ojibwe) forced the Santee into Minnesota;
and the Teton and Yankton (from Minnesota) onto the Great Plains,
(with horse and buffalo,) what is now NORTH and SOUTH DAKOTA
where many of these people remain.

The Santee Sioux gave up land of Minnesota
for agriculture on a reservation,
(Little Crow defeated) then forced westward to Dakota and Nebraska[65]
after treaties, after white violations.

The Teton and Yankton territories
were invaded after the Gold Rush of 1849;
1865-68, Red Cloud (Oglala Sioux chief), against government attempts
for a road to Montana (across favorite hunting grounds)—
with his warriors drew a line.

The First Treaty of Fort Laramie (Wyoming), 1851
led to forts and roads on Indian territory.
Nowadays, white culture spotted with 'fast food forts',
flag-waving their franchised victory.

After U.S. defeat, acknowledged
by the Second Treaty of Fort Laramie, 1868,
the Sioux were given possession of *their* South Dakota lands
and a chance to recuperate.

But mid-1870s, when gold discovered
in the sacred Paha Sapa, Black Hills of South Dakota,
miners <u>invaded</u> the Sioux reservation
respecting the treaty—not one iota.

Then, at the Battle of Little Bighorn, 1876 (in Montana),
the Sioux (and others), and the Cheyenne
gave Lieutenant Colonel George A. Custer
his infamous last stand.

But this winning the battle
became losing the war,
when many Sioux trapped at Tongue River valley
and returned to the reservation—though not like before.

Both Sitting Bull (Tatanka Iyotanka/Iyotake,) a Hunkpapa Lakota,
                and Crazy Horse (Tashunka Witko) an Oglala Sioux
refused to surrender their bands,
though they too (as we all one day)
had *their* last stands.

Crazy Horse killed in 1877
following his surrender;
Sitting Bull escaped to Canada,
later killed resisting Indian police — 1890, December.

En route to the Oglala Lakota Nation's Pine Ridge Reservation, 1890,
the U.S. Army forced many to the creek of Wounded Knee:
a shot escaped, then, the massacres of Sioux men, women, and children
—and the whites became 'the powers that be'.

On the face of the stone of Nature's rock
the faces of presidents chiseled to display
big white brother watching over the land,
Mount Rushmore—a monument to dismay.

Colorado, Kansas, Montana, Nebraska, Wyoming
and the Dakotas...from "lands guaranteed" to the Indians of the plains,
the Treaty of Fort Laramie Wyoming
mis-treated into Capitol, or is that Capital, gains.[66]

Being sculpted a stretch from there
in stone, the Spirit of Crazy Horse;[67]
rocks are considered the original people,
you can sit on them, and contemplate your course.

North Dakota prairies reduced
by settlers by 80 percent to mostly land of crops,
affecting plant, animal, insect, soil and water—[68]
that's what happens when domination never stops.

North Dakota tribes exist today, including:
Standing Rock Sioux, Spirit Lake Sioux,
Turtle Mountain Band of Chippewa,
the Mandan, Hidatsa, Arikara Nation, and Sisseton-Wahpeton Sioux.[69]

South Dakota tribes exist today, including:
Yankton Sioux, Oglala Lakota (Sioux,) Flandreau Santee Sioux,
Rosebud Sioux, Sisseton-Wahpeton Dakota (Sioux,)
Lower Brule Sioux, Crow Creek Sioux, Cheyenne River Sioux.

North's nickname "Peace Garden State":
on the international boundary with the Canadian province of Manitoba,
the International Peace Garden also touches
the Allies-land, DAKOTA.

29th – 1846 – IOWA

Before the territory, the river;
before the river, the ancestors, then the IOWAY
between the Mississippi and Missouri rivers
"the land between two rivers" some say.

Or, a teasing nickname from their Sioux kin: "the sleepy ones"
                                        the Ayuhwa[70], (Ai'yuwe)
and probably not "this is the place", "beautiful land".
Or, Otoe-Chiwere; Ioway-Chikiwere "The People Who Are From Here"
meaning "the original people of this place"—
                        and where true Iowans no longer stand.

But they call themselves Baxoje(BAH-khoh-jay) or Pahodje which means
"ashy-grey snow-covered heads"
from an Otoe tease, when the wind blew
the ash and snow over their heads.[71]

Other tribes were forced onto Iowa hunting grounds
then, treaty-after-U.S.-treaty diminished land,
though the Iowa tribe of Kansas and Nebraska
and the Iowa tribe of Oklahoma still stand.

When the Quapaw(h) did not cross the river,
they went the "downstream" way,
but crossing the Missouri,
the Omaha ("upstream") and also the Ioway.

89

They traveled around by seasons.
They suffered warfare as other tribes were forced west.
Today we know IOWA for soybeans and corn.
The original people survive—though forced to fly from their nest.

28th – 1845 – TEXAS

Mexican independence from Spain in 1821,
then, after the 1835-36 War, 'Texas' broke from despotic Mexico
with Davy Crockett and the "Lone Star Republic"
discouraging black citizenship. In 1901 – Texaco.

Mexico split from Spain, 1821,
Texas split from Mexico, 1836
but don't feel sorry for the "Lone Star logo"—
this land really a tribal mix.

In a state sometimes known for approved executions,
and the rigging of oil from the ground where it spills,
thanks to Lady Bird Johnson's Highway Beautification Act
you can drive past the tulips and daffodils.

TEXAS from the Caddo Confederacy—
Tejas, Teysas, or Techas "ALLIES or FRIENDS";
now oil men and cowboys, cattle and leather
ride on the range, or around the bends.

"Teysha" 'hello friend' in Caddo language (a greeting between allies),
how Indians then Spanish would refer to friendly tribes
throughout Texas, Louisiana, Arkansas and Oklahoma—
a name to remember good vibes.

Kadahadacho, along the Red River, a "real chief";
and Hasinai "our own people or culture";
whose lands were allotted and 'trusted' by government,
by the 1901 Dawes Act (Indian Allotment Act) - a legislative vulture.

A civilized people, culturally advanced, a blending (most likely)
of Mississippian culture with earthen temple mounds...
Caribbean migrations to the Gulf Coast before 500 A.D.—
themselves growing maize, beans and squash within home bounds.

Gulf coast Karankawas, and herb eating Coahuiltecan;
pueblo Patarabueyes, and horseriding Comanche;
Tonkawa and other hunter-gatherers;
Pawnee, linguistically; and Lipan- and Mescalero-Apache.

90

The Caddo also influenced by French in Louisiana,
and Mexicans in what today we call Texas,
and they now have a Nation with the Wichita in Oklahoma,
some distance... from a former some twenty-tribes nexus.

21ˢᵗ – 1818 – ILLINOIS
From how they called themselves—HILENI, ILLINIWEK, ILINWOK, or
ILLINI, "tribe of superior MEN", the French rendered ILLINOIS,
a vigorous, populous southern Algonquian Nation,
 the French and Canadian "found":
a confederation of tribes—man, woman, girl and boy.

Yet, related to the Delaware,
remember the LENNI LENAPE,
thus, Ils-LENNI-uois[72]
they are "Real Men" too, as the French could well see.

Of Cahokia, Kaskaskia, Michigamea, Moingwena,
Peoria, Tamaroa, Miami, and Illinois (loosely listed,)
on lands known today as Missouri, Wisconsin, and Iowa
this Illinois Confederacy consisted.

La Salle traveled down the Mississippi,
came across a river with tribes living near,
(en route to claiming Louisiana)
he named the waters for the people here.

In Cahokia, Illinois
a pyramidal structure rivaling Mexico and Egypt today,
and that tells you something about the Mississippian culture
and the land upon which they once had sway.

19ᵗʰ – 1816 – INDIANA
For the INDIAN lands
whose limestone helped build the Pentagon,
U.S. Treasury, Empire State Building, Rockefeller Center;
the rock was shipped out by the ton

for numerous state capitols and government buildings.
Lots more forest before the pioneers,
now fewer "Indians";[73]
and a government built on arrears.

More miles of interstate highway
per square mile than any other state.
"Crossroads of America" & the Indy (not the Fortune)
500, at the going rate.

James Dean born here, Abe Lincoln moved here, long after
the winning of the French-British-Indian wars. To the British legion,
(with the Treaty of Paris, 1763)
France surrendered claims to the lower Great Lakes region.

The name adopted for Indiana Territory, most likely
from a tract of land ceded by Indians in Pennsylvania.[74]
There were pre-historic communities some 15,000 years ago;
and tribes, when Europeans arrived with unresolved battle-mania.

Land of the Indians, INDIANA,
might have been THE name for the United States,
with the Indians' *own* 'amendments' for selected 'settlers'
only *then* becoming 'American' Indians,
                    by *earning* their way, through time-worn gates.

'Indiana' (and other states) paid money for Indian scalps.
So, yet another myth to dis-spell,
of ONLY the Indians scalping white men's locks—
another historical pell-mell.

        This beauteous place—
        the Red Race call Turtle Island.
        And the lesson remains—you can buy
        but you cannot own land!

How often have 'the settlers'
left so many 'unsettled'?
Yet nonetheless a home is made
'round heart, 'round hearth, 'round kettle.

        Deep inside....
        the Center of one's being
        Contemplate Creator, or,
        Universal seeing.

        Carries the World
        upon Her back
        Balancing the steady
        and the fast track.

        Wise old Turtle
        of Longevity,
        carries the weight
        of our brevity.

The Turtle lifts us
on Her shell,
and so, our global stories
tell.

Hindu myths
and those Chinese,
American Indian
and Australian Aborigines.

This beauteous Earth
so many call Turtle Island
and the lesson remains—you can buy,
but you must caretake land!

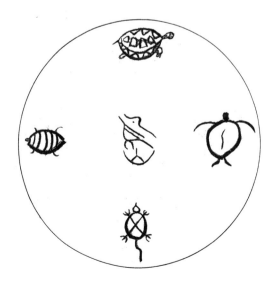

OF EARTH (mostly)

"EARTH"

T'U
The two layers [horizontal]:
[top]-"crust" or "soil", &
[bottom] "subsoil"..
from which all
"growing things" [vertical]
are born.

This solid turf that spans the globe
held in the hand is reduced to dirt.
How solid, how fragile;
how much more absorbing the hurt?

Splendid soil of various textures
from hard-packed plains to sandy loam,
across oceans, continents, nations and other prisons,
the *only* place we call terrestrial home.

From mountain, meadow, hill and dirt-road,
and on down to grassy patch,
from planetary body, star, and spaceship:
Earth—the *only* place our feet would catch.

And the African-Americans, used as slaves,
when the Indians would no longer suffice,
ALL helped build the fabric of this country
with Whites and Asians and others—each one can give advice.

Respect and befriend all of the races
by at least Understanding if you don't agree,
for each of the races is a reflection of Self
and a part of the wholeness Spiritually, Mentally and Planetarily.

Conquer and befriend your Shadowy-self,
Purify the impurities of your Duality-self,
Activate the fullness of your Whole-self,
Attain the perfection of your Highest-self.

6ᵗʰ – 1788 – MASSACHUSETTS

Massachuset tribe "AT THE RANGE OF HILLS"
the white men are coming, they probably knew.
Liberty battles, Tea party, now the Commonwealth:
the British came too.

For the blueberries[75], Great Blue Hill Region south of Boston,
where the tribe once lived overlooking the bay,
or farther north, "small mountain or hill place" Massa Wachusett —
that's what some people say.

"AT or ABOUT THE LARGE HILL PLACE" MASSACHUSETTS.
At Plimoth Plantation, the "People of the First Light" Wampanoag,
and Pawtucket and Nipmuck...then the "floating island" Mayflower
                              with Pilgrims arrived and though industrious
on the great wheel they were only a cog,

though the Puritans proceeded to affect a culture
and their mores and conservatism still lingers,
but only for those so righteous
who *only* at church are singers.

Rising above dapper, prudish crossed-legs
and embodying more of the true Jesus,
the Transcendentalists sparked a new age of being:
putting together the oft scattered pieces.

Through Nature and the outdoor temple
they found spirits hitherto tied to the church:
see the bird on the wing, see the grass-blade and sing
for the meek though they're left in the lurch.

"HILL"
a slope with
        steps
&
slope, steps,
and forest
[**O**s] on top

For within the white birch
and the bird on his perch,
you'll find the spiritual mover way down low,
or up high—if you search!

One meek man named Ghandi saw a clearing
in the political woods that were dense,
inspired by the likes of Emerson and Thoreau
to acts of civil disobedience.

Before the material the spiritual—
the basic message of Transcendentalists,
though a tough one for the land-grabbers
who'd rather be shaking their fists.

Whatever works to help you transcend
any problems of earthly injustice
is a feather in the cap of transcendental philosophy
and a thorn for the boomers and bust-uhs.

There were Salem witch trials
where they burned at the stake,
yet magic, and gatherings, and forests, and pathways live on—
(once the Massachusetts Bay Colony) and the Boston beans still bake.

Most of the poor and farming types
were not satisfied with the Constitution-for-the-wealthy's forming days;
see the 1780s Shay's Rebellion
led by army veteran Daniel Shays.

13th – 1790 – RHODE ISLAND
"State of RHODE ISLAND and Providence of Plantations"
the smallest state with the longest official name,
home of The Narragansett Indian Tribe,
        descendants of aboriginal peoples
(over 30,000 years ago) from whence they came.

Their stories visible on the faces both
of rock formations and the people's word-of-mouth.
Narragansett, an English corruption of Nanhigganeuck,
Dutch Nahican, "people of the small point"[76] of spirit routh.

First documented contact was in 1524
by visitor Giovanni da Verrazano
who recorded an island about the size of Rhodes of Greece,
though *he* came from Florence, not Milano.

Rhode, a Greek goddess of the Isle of Rhodes
and wife of sun-god Helios:
was she a beacon for the likes of sailors
Verrazano and famed Odysseus?

With land purchased from the Narragansett,
the colony founded by Roger Williams and religious refugees in 1636,
fleeing Puritanism on the Massachusetts Bay Colony
where they weren't getting their kicks.

A haven for outcasts,
Quakers, Jews,
and those defying moral precepts
for a particular inner faith to choose.

Williams also founded the town of Providence
and spoke of "soul-liberty";
he was a friend to tribal chiefs—
Roger's Island, more appropriately.

For the last colony to ratify the Constitution,
the shipbuilding industry went hand-in-hand
with privateering:
hence the nickname, Rogue's Island.

Also known for the Rhode Island Red
and Newport's high-society mansions,
both a form of domestic fowl
near vast coastlines and vistaed expansions.

And once the home of General Nathaniel Greene,
George Washington's revolutionary right-hand-man,
a respected 'native' who was also a Quaker—
though his juggling of war and peace is tough to understand.

Considered now a worldly sailing capitol,
and another theory poses this much:
"Roodt(e) Eylandt" 'Red Island' for the red clay lining the shore,
by another explorer, Adriaen Block (Block Island), a Dutch.

22nd – 1819 – ALABAMA

"THICKET-CLEARERS", "VEGETATION GATHERERS"
from the Upper Creek Confederacy,
the indigenous tribes Albam-Coushatta
how a name carries on you'll see.

Both moved to Texas to avoid more battles—
Coushatta (Koasati) probably "white cane or reed",
and the Alibamus, "gardening and clearing" trails,
gave the Koasati homeless a home, after a forgotten deed.[77]

A combination of Choctaw words, Alba ayamute "I clear the thicket"
"alba" 'vegetation, herbs, plants'
and "amo" 'gatherer, picker'
"alba-amo"—through thickets advance.[78]

"TO GATHER"

three hands
picking herbs

Alibamo (sub-tribe of Creek)
    from areas Mississippi to Louisiana and Alabama to Texas,
cultures of villagers and farmers forced from the land
                    but their spirits soared higher;
Coushatta from Tennessee river, to Louisiana and Georgia, to Texas—
both of moundbuilding temples, and keepers of the sacred fire.[79]

Four of the most influential African-Americans
followed these tribal-name patterns:
Booker T. Washington, George Washington Carver, Martin L. King Jr.—
"cleared" then "gathered".

In Montgomery, Alabama, 1955
spontaneously on a bus,
a 'law-abiding' bus driver
attempted to make a fuss.

> "MILLET or PLANTS"
> above "Water/Moisture"
> also
> "Sticky" Plants

This seminal moment for the Civil Rights Movement
occurred when a seamstress, Rosa Parks refused to move
while on her way home from work that day,
she said (though a bit tired)—she had nothing to prove.

Legend has it Alabama is an Indian word
meaning "here we (may) rest",[80]
but the Creek "Battle of Horseshoe Bend" with Pres. Jackson
was anything but-- triggering his policy of forcing Indians west.

Limamu or Alibamu or Alabamas or Alibamons
ALABAMA also called "Tribal Town"[81]
where the Tuskegee Institute,
and the Civil Rights Movement were found.

44th – 1890 –WYOMING
From a Delaware word "mountains and valleys alternating"
and the Wyoming Valley, PA,
which was the site of a revolutionary massacre
though the name traveled away.

"WATER"

Actually, Lenape for "Susquehanna"
meaning 'water crossing a big plain',
"mee-chay-wee-ah-meeing(k)".[82] And from old maps,
'the people of the place where water crosses the plain'.

A publisher named Freeman claimed it was he
who suggested the name for part of the Dakota territory,
"mscheweamiing" from Dakota, "at the big flats or large plains"—
according to his story.

M'cheuwomink, became Chiwaumuc, Wiawamic,
Wayomic, Waiomink, then WYOMING.[83]
If you're quiet enough.....
the sounds of water crossing the big-plains..sing.

"FIELD"

Wind River Reservation,
third largest in the U.S.A.,
home to Eastern Shoshone(i) and Northern Arapaho(e)
today.

Eastern Shoshone by way of Nevada-Utah
around the year 1600 onto the Great Plains;
around Little Big Horn times, the Arapaho forced
onto Shoshone reservation where they remain.

Once *they* were enemies
and now are side by side,
separate cultures
on joint land, still wide—

though not nearly as wide
as once it had been,
due to gold mining, as we've seen,
again and again.

Big Wind River, Little Wind River
water-courses through the reservation,
maintaining the traditional ways
overcoming attempted soul-excavation.

Rewriting frontier history would read
NOT how the west was won,
but how many tribes fled or were forced there
preserving their culture on the run.

WYOMING wide-open,
with many a rancher's face;
Yosemite, Grand Tetons, birthplace of Black Elk(Oglala Sioux holy man,)
"WATER on the LARGE PLAINS PEOPLE'S PLACE."

41st – 1889 – MONTANA

Most well known for Yellowstone Park (also in Idaho and Wyoming)
and a faithful geyser. Buffalo still roam
on the Bison Range. To the Confederated Salish and Kootenai Tribes
of the Flathead Indian Reservation—a home.

Early on there was lots of mining,
though nary a mention of gold,
with plenty of copper, and lead, and zinc,
and silver, oil and coal.

Part of the land from Lewis and Clark was acquired,
part from France, and part from Great Britain,
Louisiana Purchase, 1803, and Oregon Treaty, 1846—
nowadays plenty of streams for trout fishin'.

Gold discovered, 1863. Then, created out of Idaho territory, 1864,
Big Sky country MONTANA,
where many a ranch-hand (originally the Kiowa) works the land
so they don't wait around for manna.

Chosen from a Latin dictionary by J.M. Ashley
"montaanus" 'mountainous', actually Spanish "montaña",
with lots of hearty grains on the plains
a good place to wear a bandana.

"MOUNTAIN"

Blackfeet People at the foot of the mountain.
Crow tribe, really "Apsaalooke" 'children of the large-beaked bird'.[84]
Plus, other tribes banded without a land to call home
remaining connected, though not often heard.

Sioux tribes gathered
at the Little Bighorn River,
and the infamous battle ensued--
for land, at the cost of human liver.

45th – 1896 – UTAH
Before the Franciscans
and the arrival of the Spanish horse,
before the Mexicans, Mormons, Europeans,
and U.S., of course

the five major tribes with bands
through mountains, plains, desert, valleys and basins,
the Paiute, Goshute, Dine' (Navaho), and,
Shoshoni and Ute Nations.[85]

Spanish "Yutas", Shoshoni "Yuuta"
"PEOPLE of the MOUNTAINS" UTAH,
for the "higher up" Ute—
a tribe well-known for their chutzpah.

"MOUNTAIN"

(And before all of them, the Uto-Aztecan speaking,
and the Anasazi ('Ancient Ones'), and some before them.)
Eventually The Five Tribes were forced off lands, enduring massacres,
and yes, even an Executive Order by President A. Lincoln

100

sending some to the farthest corner of the state,
the Uintah-Ouray Reservation, around 1861,
yet the tribes survive and some, like the Ute Mountain Ute's
Reservation of Colorado, Utah, and New Mexico
                          earn money from pottery and gambling fun.

There's a special Salt Lake
where you float not swim,
be you married, single,
lesbian, gay, or multiple-wives-Mormon,

or one of Five Tribes on Olympic ice
ceremoniously in 2002:
the Ute Nation, the Shoshoni Nation,
the Paiute, the Dine'(Navaho), and the Goshute, too.

49th – 1959 – ALASKA

Probably, Unangan(Aleut) "THAT WHICH THE SEA BREAKS AGAINST",
"mainland", AGUNALAKSH, AL-AY-EK-SA, or AL-AK-SHAK,
a Russian variation made ALASKA:
last refuge of wilderness—let's not track!

Four main peoples have caretaken
a delicate balance of mountain, land and sea,
Unangan(Aleut), Inuit(Eskimo), Athapaskans,
and Northwest Coast Indians inlcuding the Tlingit..
                          spanning Alaskan territory.

"WATER" [left] &
"ISLES" [o]
surrounded by
water[curvy lines]

This land invaded by Russian monarchy,
and the Church of Russian Orthodox
and though fur trade disruptive they enhanced bilingual literacy,
and blended with the culture where the sea..... rocks.

Numerous subgroups of Unangan people
surviving forced relocations and slavery,
and though not considered "Indians"
these "Natives" (called Aleuts by the Russians) still manifest bravery.

Seal pelts, and sea otter sold with many going to China.
After 125 year rule— in 1867, Alaska sold by Russia to the U.S.;
yet Inuit, Unangan, Athabascan, and Indians there
(and in Canada) long before—didn't anybody bother to discuss?

U.S. outlawed the Unangan language, and for gold, oil, and uranium
many originals were re-located;
now environmentalists and others help protect the land
against pure profiteers—and celebrate the emancipated.

101

A blanket-scape of frigid wilderness,
white-capped land of the midnight sun,
laden with oil. Back off! Choose electric! Hydrogen! Solar!...
let the polar bear and caribou freely run.

Perhaps the *first* Americans, Asian
from Siberia across a land bridge, 13-40,000 yrs ago,
                              (now the Bering Strait,)
hunting mammoths, bison and stags...
Long, long before there was even one 'state'.

50th – 1959 – KA PAE `AINA HAWAI`I LOA = Hawaiian Nation or, HAWAII to the U.S. government

The last, (so far),
HAWAII, a spiritual AND physical abode,
Hawai'i from Hawai'iki, a Polynesian mythical-homeland pathway
what American Indians call "The Good Red Road".

Of volcanic origin, with eight main islands,
the oldest formed 6 million years ago.
Kanaka Hawai'i Maoli, "the Real People" the Natives call themselves,
surviving U.S. enforced colonialism, and a world volcano that can blow.

For the Earl of Sandwich, Captain Cook said:
"Sandwich Islands" in 1778.
Some say a fisherman named Hawai`iloa discovered,
though some won't take *that* bait.

KA PAE'AINA O HAWAI'I LOA:
on Cook's Island called "`Avaiki"; in Aotearoa "Hawaiki";
Tahiti's name "Havai`i" (now "Ra`iatea"); to Samoa "Savai`i".[86]
Some say homeland Owhyhee—where the truth burns bright as a tiki.

Some say a combination of "Hawa" 'traditional homeland'
and "ii" 'raging'-like a volcano, or 'new or small'.[87]
On several islands to preserve the beauty,
no buildings built higher than palm trees, 80 feet tall.

From roadside farms and tropical rainforests
a most mouth-watering list on the planet:
papaya, pineapple, lemons, limes,
oranges and pomegranate,

star fruit, passion fruit, grapefruit, breadfruit,
mountain apple, mango, and guava,
macadamia nut, coconut, coffee from Kona—
keep a heads up for the lava!

Originally with no concept
of privately owned land,
the plight of the Kanaka Hawai'i Maoli
you must try to understand:

See "The Apology Resolution" passed by Congress
signed by President Clinton, November 23, 1993,
to repair the conspiracy and "overthrow of the indigenous and lawful"
government of the Kingdom of Hawaii.[88]

This beauteous place—
the Red Race call Turtle Island
and the lesson remains—you can buy
but you cannot own land.

And the names and the people
live on with grace,
first named from what
they saw or lived nearby

of earth
and of the flowing waters
upon which
the people steered by.

Carries a protective shell,
four legs like four directions,
sticks Her neck out, or,
goes inside, protections.

When on land
outruns the hare.
Deep inside...
the gifts of Prayer.

Carries the World
upon Her back,
Balancing the steady
and the fast track

the Turtle
lifts us on Her shell,
and so, our global stories
tell.

To the underworld through water
for a ball of earth.....
emerging again—
a worldly re-birth.

Soft clumps of dirt
upon Her hard back shell.....
a landing pad
for those who fell.

This beauteous earth
so many call Turtle Island,
and the lesson remains—you can buy
but you must caretake land!

And the African-Americans, used as slaves,
when the Indians would no longer suffice,
ALL helped build the fabric of this country
with Whites and Asians and others—each one can give advice.

Respect and befriend all of the races
by at least Understanding if you don't agree,
for each of the races is a reflection of Self
and a part of the wholeness Spiritually, Mentally and Planetarily.

Conquer and befriend your Shadowy-self,
Purify the impurities of your Duality-self,
Activate the fullness of your Whole-self
Attain the perfection of your Highest-self.

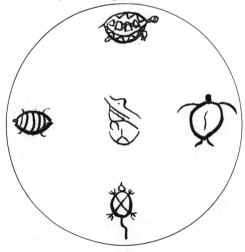

4
OF SPANISH (mostly)

The Spanish-American(&Cuban War,) 1898,
for big business domination;
"The People" ignored— while timber, sugar, railroading,
                                        minerals, etc. stored
for imperial marketing sensation

and Puerto Rico, Philippines,
Guam, Wake Island and Hawaii — annexations;
a 'manifest destiny' in all directions
lacking ratiocinations.[89]

27th – 1845 – FLORIDA

While searching for the "Fountain of Youth"
Ponce de Leon got tropical showers;
in 1513, he gave 'la FLORIDA' its name
                        (1st seen on Palm Sunday)
on Pasqua de Flores, "Flowery Easter" or "Feast of Flowers".

The land had been semi-permanently settled
by Indians, as far back as 800 B.C.;
now known for oranges and grapefruits
sweet and sour, yet very juicy.

"FLOWER"
(see p.31)

But aside from the fountain of youth
Ponce de Leon sought to capture slaves for Hispaniola;[90]
he thought Indians were as easy to pick
as a bunch of African gladiola.

The state claimed by France and England
then once again by Spain,
until at last sold
to the United States in 1819.

The Seminole War of 1818
led to Florida as part of America's gain,
and the Florida Purchase of 1819
was the result of Andrew Jackson's military campaign.

Runaway slaves (Black Seminoles,) and Creek (Muskokee) Indians,
and Calusas (islanders) migrated to the 'flowery' lands:
where they're known (including the Timcua) as the Seminole (Siminoli)—
overall, a history with many hands.

The Seminole though heavily outnumbered
held fast (until the 1840s) to Florida's swampy terrain,
yet tired after an 8 year war, they emerged under truce flags!
...only to be arrested again, and again.

"The Last and Only
Fully Sovereign Nation in North America", they claim to be—
the Miccosukee Seminole Nation;[91] Chief Osceola, in 1837 captured,
while a white truce flag was waving—very dirty.

31st – 1850 – CALIFORNIA

Califia or Calafia a mythical, paradisal land
and a Queen of the Amazons from an early 16th century book,
a Spanish romance by Garcia Ordóñez de Montalvo—
then Hollywood became the hook.

Or, Arabic (and Spanish) "caliph" from '(k)halifa'
generic term for Islamic successor[92]; or, Latin "calida fornax"
'hot furnace' region
where farm workers bend their backs.

Or, "cal y forno" from Indians 'lime kiln' (like calc);
Forno del Cal a 'salt mine' 'oven of the whitewash',
lime, water and glue makes a whitewash;
or, to gloss over blemishes, how posh!

Or, KALI FORNO from Baja Indians
"native land, or mountains, or high hills",
where numerous tribes did and still live
existing without many frills.

And a professor George Davidson poses
etymologically from two Greek words,
CALIFORNIA has another derivation
from "beauty" and from "birds".[93]

By 1773, the Spanish mission system
virtually wiped out 300 Southern Indian bands,[94]
by forcing a so-called god upon them—
that's not a god I could ever understand.

From the 1590s the Spanish,
from 1821 the amenable Mexicans,
and in 1850 the United States of America
finally tipped the pans.

106

Gold discovered– 1848; gold rush 1849;
in 1850 a state—you do the math:
steep cliffs, rock shores, redwoods—just don't forget
Ishi, Steinbeck and *The Grapes of Wrath.*

The gold rush's living legacy
is mercury dumped into the rivers,
for "gold", for "greed", for "genocide"—95
pure propaganda to call the Red race "Indian givers."

And, 1848 Treaty of Guadalupe Hidalgo
ended the Mexican war,
so California was ceded to the U.S.
         along with west Colorado and New Mexico,
Texas, Arizona, Nevada, and Utah—that's a big score!

Anglo California split from Mexico
forming the "Bear Flag Republic"
then threatened the native Indians.
What happened to Plato's "Republic"?

Before the City of Angels
was a hot spot for tourist seeing,
there lived the Tongva or Gabrielino, people who bowed to Quaoar—
a force of nature that brought forth all other beings.

Beneath L.A. smog and Hollywood tinsel,
above New Age fads and cemented stars—
voices for Nature and The Way,
Mt. Shasta, G. Snyder, Ferlinghetti....amidst endless cars.

St. Francis for the birds and critters;
be glad for your little portion.
San Francisco's gay, and City Lights,
a long, long list of tribes..... and Haight-Asbury's drug absorption.

From a Spanish romance novel
to the mission of Church lovers,
by 1770s over 300 Indian bands near extinction—
'no judging books by their covers.'

36th – 1864 – NEVADA
Spanish sea sailors saw
California mountains off the coast.
A new territory carved from Utah—
where horseless croupiers now play host.

Sierra NEVADA "SNOWY RANGE or CAPPED"
with a desert and mountains.
Las Vegas, gambling capitol—
bright lights and bubbling fountains.

A place for drive-thru marriages
and legal sex-undressin',
and heck, why not, it's only fair—
the oldest known profession!

From "SNOW-CLAD" peaks
it's a bit of a trip,
to scantily clad dancers
and tourists peeking at the "Strip",

and the promise, no...possibility
of striking it rich,
though 'odds' on that are minimal
in the playground full of glitz.

A gambling addiction is really only
attempting to control one's fate;
a sublimated way of gaming like a child
and arriving at a spiritual state.

And for various tribes
casinos are a way,
to earn back some money
taken from them by the U.S. of A.

From NEVADA the lesson of being "SNOW-CLAD"—
protected and clothed by nature's purity,
a symbolic trusting of one's feet on the path
and making peace with bright obscurity.

38th – 1876 – COLORADO
Between southwest Indian and northerly rancher,
COLORADO "COLOR RUDDY or RED"
for rivers and windblown sandstones;
once a gold rush—now legalized gambling instead.

After gold discovered and treaties ignored
the Sand Creek Massacre, in November 1864,
of Cheyenne and Arapaho--
how unCivil any war.

Outside on mountains skiers soar
past spruce and ponderosa pine,
'cross vast enchanted wilderness
and still, the state flower flowers, in beauteous shades –
                                        the scarred columbine.

On deep-blue skies in thin-crisp air
quaking aspen, golden, shake;
and carved inside Cheyenne mountain
(NORAD) North American Aerospace Defense Commanders watch...
                                        for a mistake.

Rocky Mountain's adolescent peaks
stretch across this beauteous terrain,
where Indian paintbrush, a red-orange flower.....
dots a canvas welcoming rain.

    And the names and the people
    live on with grace,
    first named from what
    they saw or lived nearby

    of earth
    and of the flowing waters
    upon which
    the people steered by.

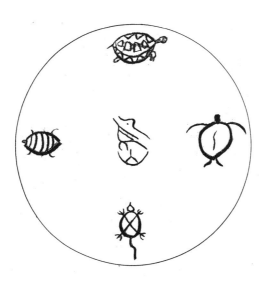

5
OF MEXICAN (mostly)

Henry David Thoreau spent one night in jail, 1846,
for refusing to pay taxes for the Mexican War;
two years later with a "Civil Disobedience" lecture—
he opened a non-violent door.

47th – 1912 – NEW MEXICO

By Spaniards from Mexico in the 16th century,
NEW MEXICO for land north and west of the Rio Grande,
"land of enchantment" and aptly so
for places like Roswell, extra-terrestrial and manned.

A culture of Anglos and Hispanics,
Ute, Navaho, Jicarilla and Mescalero Apache, and Europeans;
with some of the most beautiful vistas,
if you get a chance go see 'em.

NUEVO MEXICO, from MEXICO, an Aztec name,
a title of Huitzilopochtli's, a warrior-god:
"place of Mexitli", or, "hare of the aloes" —
perhaps a medicinal healer when times were hard.

"Mexitli" probably Huitzilopochtli's name
and, "co" 'where it is',
thus, the place of the Eagle-god[96]
and those that followed the culture that was his.

Also "metzti" 'the moon',
and, "xi(r)(c)tli" 'center, navel, or a hare'
'one in the center of the moon'
the foundation of that culture there.[97]

(Mayan and American Indian peoples
also see a rabbit in the moon,
perhaps the inspiration for trickster and healer
Bugs Bunny and his looney tune.)

And, "metl" 'maguey' a Mexican aloe plant
for healing, and hemp or mescal intoxications,[98]
like Christ with wine, the Anointed one,
some of Huitzilopochtli's ramifications.

Mythologically, the son of the sun and moon,
a god of the house of dawn who begins hunting stars,[99]
portraying the path from night to day, and night again—
a journey from here to afar.

For the feathers worn on his left leg,
Huitzilopochtli also "humming-bird to the left";
dance joyfully as a peaceful warrior
and the bird-god will claim you deft.

Home of numerous Pueblos
and their wise, ancient folk,
with pottery bearing 'spiral of life' and 'altar steps' symbols
                                    all the way to Lemuria
where THE first race awoke.

Though conquistadored and churchified
Pueblo traditions have not slept;
mud-and-straw adobe poor in appearance,
though by Spirit—well-kept!

Along with Navaho and Apache, only 19 of 90+ Pueblo villages remain:
Acoma, Cochiti, Jemez, Nambe, Picuris,
                    Pojoaque, Sandia, San Felipe, Isleta,
San Ildefonso, San Juan, Santa Ana, Santa Clara, Santa Domingo,
Taos, Tesuque, Zia, Zuni(reservation), and Laguna.

        And the names and the people
        live on with grace,
        first named from what
        they saw or lived nearby,

        of earth
        and of the flowing waters
        upon which
        the people steered by.

        This beauteous place
        the Indians call Turtle Island
        and the lesson remains—you can claim
        buy you cannot own land!

And the African-Americans, used as slaves,
when the Indians would no longer suffice,
ALL helped build the fabric of this country
with Whites and Asians and others—each one can give advice.

Respect and befriend all of the races
by at least Understanding if you don't agree,
for each of the races is a reflection of Self
and a part of the wholeness Spiritually, Mentally and Planetarily.

Conquer and befriend your Shadowy-self,
Purify the impurities of your Duality-self,
Activate the fullness of your Whole-self
Attain the perfection of your Highest-self

      Carries the World
      upon Her back,
      Balancing the steady
      and the fast track

      This beauteous earth
      so many call Turtle Island,
      and the lesson remains—you can buy
      but you must caretake land!

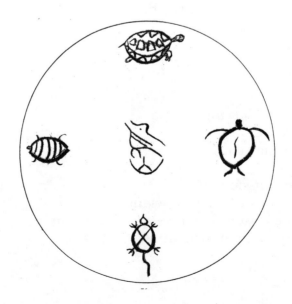

6
OF ENGLISH (mostly)

Give thanks to the monarch who started it all,
George III, the infamous despotic King,
for helping bring forth declarations of freedoms—
only for *those* do we Sing!

America as refuge for the persecuted
but some folks the fault perpetuated,
capitalizing on a change of scenery
forgetting they were 'newly' emancipated.

Hitler and Stalin along with various ills
were both physically beaten by their fathers;
what inferiority! what dis-pleasure!
revenged on innocent others.

11th – 1788 – NEW YORK
'NEW' YORK from English for a Duke of York and Albany,
probably from British "york": 'wild boar', OR, estate with 'YEW-tree',[100]
first, New Netherland (and Amsterdam), with mountains and islands...
then skyscrapers, finance, Broadway, Statue of Liberty.

That 'Duke', James Stuart, also Earl of Ulster,
of the lineage of Kings Charles, and James of Bible translation;
'Duke' a title going back to Rome
and bearing a monarch and military affiliation,

then affecting New York, New Jersey,
the Carolinas and Maryland,
with namesakes and prestige
to strike-up-the-band.

Peter Minuit 'dealt' for NY with tribes
with whom fair trading was busy;
beaver pelts and wampum for European goods
the start of the industrious city.

The British took 'New' Amsterdam
 (including a wall to keep the Lenape out,)
from then anti-semite, Peter Stuyvesant[101], and the Dutch.
On Wall St., what was once a slave market, now a stock market,
but at least, the low-income slave-workers (except in pockets)
 they can't touch.

At a vital port of entry to New York
who could best do the manual labor?
Blacks, whites, mulattos and Indians
for the shipping biz then in favor.

With a British assault on New York
in 1776,
many black slaves were defense
though many had joined the Brits.

And G. Washington, strong with 18,000 soldiers
at the Battle of Long Island, then retreated
to Manhattan, and after 6 years of war and British control,
only then (1781) with a 'promise'—was slavery defeated.

On July 4th of 1827,
a proclamation of no-slavery,
though it wasn't until 1841
that the proclamation manifested its bravery.

And except for some slaves coming in on some ships
it was 1865 before the law was fully polished.
It took a Civil War (600,000 killed) and a 13th amendment
to have slavery fully abolished!

And a large population of Jewish people
escaping from Nazi incarceration;
plus many Italian, Irish, and European, Asian, Hispanic, Latino,
and others, now call this land their nation.

But before all of THAT,
before the big sell,
Lenape Hoking "The Dwelling-Place of the Lenape", or
E-hen-da-wi-kih-tit "Where the Ordinary People Dwell".[102]

And before all of THAT,
before the tallest skyscrapers (scaled by Mohawk) were seen,
there were villages and pathways, and
Yes, even Manhattan...once grassy green!

Remember the Delaware?
Make that the LENAPE and the truth you will tell,
of the first inhabitants, pre-Columbian, pre-concrete, nobody special:
E-hen-da-wi-kih-tit "Where the Ordinary People Dwell".

NY home to The League of Iroquois Nations,
in their own tongue Hau de no sau nee "People of the long house"
(or Ongwe-Oweh "original men") originators of
The Great Law of Peace![103]
and, like the Cherokee and others, a matrilineal society, headed by
the matriarchal spouse.

Women owned property and determined kinship,
each clan headed by a clan mother,
each tribe—of Turtle, Bear and Wolf, with leaders chosen by the women,
and Crane, Snipe, Hawk, Beaver, Deer, and others.

Mohawk, Ganeagaono or Kahniakehake "People of the Flint",
within the League, "Keepers of the Eastern Door".
Each tribe—like the Cherokee—
has had a chief for Peace, and a chief for war.

SLOPE with
STONES or
BOULDERS

Oneida, Onyota'a:ka "Granite People, of the Standing Stone".
Onondaga "Keepers of the Wampum and the center Council Fire",
or, Ononda'gega (Onontakeka) "People on the Hills and of the
Mountains"
they compromised themselves to better the tribal choir.

Cayuga "People of the Mucky Landing or Great Swamp"
Gayogoho:no "where the boats are taken out"
or "People of the Pipe"…..
the essences of what their lives are about.

Seneca "Great Hill People with bark canoes", Nundawaono,
or, Onodowahgah,
now also the Seneca Nation of Indians "Keepers of the Western Door".[104]
"Brother, the Great Spirit has made us all…"
said Red Jacket, Sagoyewatha ("He who keeps them awake")
a Peace Chief and orator.

Red Jacket (a gift from G.W.) sought for the union of ALL Indian tribes,
an uphill battle with many stops,
with G. Washington's mouth-piece, Maj. Gen. Sullivan spouting:
"…ruin of the Indian settlements and the destruction of their crops…"[105]

"Those of the Indian Hemp" or "Hemp Gatherers"
Ska-ru-ren, originally, makers of woven hemp shirts;
the very same fabric of America's first flag,
and grown by U.S. founders from the very same dirts.

bundles of HEMP
hanging to dry

Tuscarora, "Hemp-Shirt Wearing People",
                              became non-voting members in 1722.
Some left 'North Carolina' after fighting (with English colonists) a war;
the sixth in The League of Iroquois Nations—
a League that deeply influenced the writings of our "father's fore".

Questions of whom to side with:
the British, colonists, or neutral—then the subsequent war,
divided the Six Nations
like never before.

All of them still inhabit upstate villages and reservations,
though in 1680 their territories spanned far...the four directions....
they gave us long-lasting, The Great Law of Peace—
instrumental in our Constitutional inflections!

And there's a Long Island that reaches to the sea,
"land of tribute," by the Indians called Paumanauke,
a name revived by poet Whitman—
still inhabited by the Montauk, Mattinecock, Poospatuck
                              and Shinnecock.

In Algonquian, "Sewanhacky" 'the place of shells',
or Matouac for "young man or warriors" on the isle's west side,[106]
and the Island shaped like a fish or whale,
proportionally long though not very wide.

Once there were 13 different tribes
or perhaps simply bands or various clans,
each with a name describing the nature
of the surroundings of their ancient lands.

Nissequogue "Clay Country",
Rockaway "Sandy Land",
Setaukets "Land at the Mouth of a River",
Shinnecock "People of the Shore" ("At the Level Land".)

Unkechaug/Unquachaug "People (or Land) Beyond the Hill"
Secatogue "Black or Colored Land",
Matinecock "Place to Hunt, or, Broken-Up Ground",
Manhasset "Island Sheltered by Other Islands",

Massapequa "Large Shallow Road",
Canarsie "At the Fenced-in Place", or, "Grassy Place",
Corchaug "Ancient Ones" or "Principal Place",
Montauk "Fortified Place",

Merrick "Plains Country".....
Plus many roads, parks and places
that were once, and now forever
traversed by many other-same faces...[107]

3rd – 1787 – NEW JERSEY

A Duke of York, 1664, gave a patent to two gents,
to be called Nova Caesaria or 'NEW' JERSEY
after England's largest and southernmost CHANNEL ISLES
off the coast of Normandy, France & inhabited since 2000 B.C.

A little bit of Rome on the Atlantic coast
and a lot more Rome in America's entertainment,
though the Colesseum gladiators rarely get killed.
and the chariots mostly ride on the pavement.

A little bit of Rome in the Jersey name
and a lot more Rome in the government's behavior,
with excessive taxation and lavish parties
where the coin is a personal favor.

The "Garden State" (still Lenape too,) with jersey cows
and fabrics, weft-knit jerseys;
produces two-thirds of flavor additives sold in the states
off a turnpike with chemical plants and refineries.

A piece of America of William Carlos Williams,
"Paterson" the city, man, the modern epic poem,
written by a doctor and poet,
who took care of children as well as tomes

and understood: what worth dusty shelf ?
if not applied to every day's cascading waterfalls to the Sea,
and the dance of living elves and satyrs-- the 'gist of Radiance',
the Beauty of all that Be.

"Tidewater People" the Nanticoke migrated
and met up with other 'natives', the Lenni-Lenape;
today the Nanticoke Lenni-Lenape Indians
living together in New Jersey.

9th – 1788 – NEW HAMPSHIRE

A shire was a parish of the Kings and Queens
for the purpose of taxation—
the bigger the land meant the most taxes collected
much to the King (and Queen's) elation.

117

For his home county, HAMPSHIRE in England,
known for sheep and draft horses that sire,
by Capt. John Mason of Plymouth Council— though now...
for R. Frost, White Mountains, and maple—'NEW' HAMPSHIRE.

Pennacook of areas now New Hampshire, Maine, and Massachusetts.
Abenaki word "penakuk" 'at the bottom of the hill',
also known as Merrimack, from the river villages;
seafood also how they got their fill.

They blended with various other tribes
and others with them, as well,
all along a terrain ("Countrie of the Massachusets")
                           colonizer Capt. John Smith
called 'New' England (1614), with wooded dale and dell.

Up north, from the White Mountains,
origin of rivers rolling from granite hills....
through New Hampshire, Connecticut and Maine, through rivers
        the Connecticut, Pemigewasset , Winnipesaukee, Merrimack,
        Cocheco and Salmon Falls, Piscataqua, Androscoggin and Saco—
the 'Mother of Rivers' overspills.[108]

New York, New Jersey, New Hampshire, New England
that's 'News' to me and you;
the names from afar, a whitewash of lands
to the Reds who weren't given their due.

This cultural amnesia derived
from the re-naming of territories,
and though some have kept part of the original names—
many re-arranged by the Whigs and Tories.

With ever the quest for the new and improved
many pathways are lost or they're won,
and though we evolve, one could safely admit:
not much 'new' under the sun.

            And the names live on
            with stately grace,
            reminders of the people
            with different faces

            who stopped—
            and looked—
            and named the places....
            all landmarks of the human race

This beauteous place
the Red Race call Turtle Island
and the lesson remains—you can buy
but you must caretake land!

23rd – 1820 – MAINE

Next to the offshore islands,
possibly just the main-land, called MAINE.
Or, from a compliment to Queen Henrietta
who was said to own the French province, MAYNE.

Most likely though, from an English town, Maine,
the ancestral home of colonizer Sir Ferdinando Gorges,
(partner of Capt. John Mason - see New Hampshire)
he sailed for the King James I colonizing-biz.

Broadmayne and Parva Maen, towns large and small,
were named *after* the split of his ancestral land,
(as his partner Mason for Hampshire New,)
most likely, Ferdinando to honor *his* Anglo-Saxon band.[109]

Ye Province of Maine, now known for potatoes, paper products,
ship building, and blueberries (one of the tops in the nation),
lobsters and lighthouses, clams and canoes,
mainly folks visit on vacation.

Before Europeans-- the Abnaki and Etchimins, west and east
of the Penobscot river would frolic.
Abnaki "people of the dawn"
Passamaquoddy, seafaring, "People who spear and catch pollock".

Originally of the Wabanaki Confederacy,
Ab(e)naki and bands in various directions
of Maine, Vermont, New Hampshire, Massachusetts, southern Quebec,
Canada; New York, Connecticut, and westward.....
                                despite European infections.

The English aided the Iroquois,
so the Abenaki sometimes assisted by the French,
with fur trade and religion dominating interrelations
with the foreign men-of-hench.

Four main tribes of the Confederacy in Maine today,
Passamaquoddy, Maliseet, Mikmaq and Penobscot--
most of what's left of a people
who love their 'homeland' a lot.

And before all of THAT—
ancient findings of earth-red ocher, bone and stone,
of the Red Paint People--
though that's not assuredly known.

7th – 1788 - MARYLAND, 8th – 1788 – SOUTH CAROLINA, 12th –1789 – NORTH CAROLINA

Here's a kind of trinity
of three of the southern states.
MARYLAND and the CAROLINAS, NORTH and SOUTH:
a group of namesakes, with a child of mates.

Charles of England married 15 year-old Henrietta Maria,
thus, King and Queen, Charles I and Mary.
Then, merry and intelligent Charles II, the son,
toward rulership was a little bit wary.

Also, for Charles IX of France, to be called Province of Carolana
(and with an English patent to Sir Robert Heath)—
from Caroliinus, Carolus I, Latin for CHARLES,
a sort of 'dom of fief'.

A second patent to Earl of Clarendon and others,
and the official use of the name,
a shuffling of papers and an entry
into the history book of fame.

So one might say: King 'Carlous I' for the North,
Queen 'Mary' (daughter of King Henry IV of France) for Mary-land,
King 'Carolus II' for the South,
and a good ol' family planned.

This "Colonye of men...professing the true religion"
of "culture...merchandising...&...industry...
but some parts inhabited by certain Barbarous men
who have not any knowledge of the Divine Dietye..."[110]

One can see this very attitude
in modern religio-politico-corporate domination,
with narrow-minds, greed and plutocratic "progress"
attempting to limit liberation.

The center of both Indian and African slavery
was the state of South Carolina,
and Charleston shipped natives
to the West Indies where the weather was fine-uh.[111]

On the grounds of North Carolina
the first U.S. gold supposedly found by a teen....
years later, licking his chops, and sending Cherokee from their lands
was Andrew Jackson with a habit he couldn't wean.

Yet, fond of the North's Great Smokey Mountains,
the Eastern Band of the Cherokee,
and the foothills of South Carolina
and numerous states in the vicinity.

Vital to the Indians, Chesapeake Bay
for water, fish and transportation;
the North and South Cherokees tilled and hunted
before the shaping of a nation.

Yet... MARYLAND known for Chesapeake Bay
with oysters, clams, crabs, and filet of sole,
migratory waterfowl, Lord Baltimore (George Calvert, a Catholic)
battling Susquehannock Indians— and the songster, oriole!

NORTH CAROLINA at Kitty Hawk
in 1903,
the Wright Brothers site for man's first flight
and the rest is aerial history.

SOUTH CAROLINA for cotton and tobacco,
and 137 battles through the Revolutionary War;
the beauty of many a coastal island remains,
and a ballroom dance, 'The Charleston', circa 1924.

2nd – 1787 – PENNSYLVANIA

Specified in a charter to Quaker William PENN[112]
by King Charles II around 1681,
the land a partial 'settlement' in honor of his Admiral father,
though the name would eventually also honor the son.

With a "Walking Purchase" 1737, from the Lenni Lenape
who were not pressured under the gun,
Penn's men made a deal for land—as much for as far as they could
walk in a day,
but instead (Penn had died in 1718)...they decided to run!

This sly deception and greed for land
is an apt metaphor of modern man's plight—
instead of leisurely walks and smoking a pipe
he succumbs to the instinct of fight or flight.

121

Nonetheless, Penn admired and respected the Indians,
he promoted equal rights for women as well,
and his writings and encouragement of "uncontrolled enjoyment"
preceded the Liberty Bell.

And the Indians (especially Lenape) respected *him* as well
and the "Great Treaty" and peace lasted about 70 years!
Penn wrote pamphlets, and his *Frame of Government,*
intimations of the revolutionary, Constitutional seers.

His plans for peace throughout Europe
a prototype for the U.N.
which celebrates United Nations day
on the day of the birthday of Penn.

Surprisingly, he had a few slaves,
Quakers hadn't evolved *that* far yet;
though Penn also assisted both prisoners and poor,
and had a beer brewery to keep the tongue wet.

He fostered many personal freedoms
and the structuring of state and federal laws
and the layout and shaping of cities
like a crow with higher caws.

On the whole, he understood:
that people onto this earthly plane are sent,
with an opportunity to evolve their true self—
Penn's life's work was called: the "holy experiment".

Unfortunately it was his sons and agents
who faked documents and a false deed,
that led to the "Running Purchase".
Are some still running? Indeed.

SYLVANIA "woodlands", PENNSYLVANIA
"Penn's Woodland" for peaceful Quakers, Mennonites, the Amish,
and such;
birthplace of the Constitution, with many folks from England,
Scotland, Ireland; and of German descent—the Pennsylvania Dutch.

Philadelphia, city of 'brotherly love';
Titusville first oil well; Pittsburgh, steel;
and a horse and buggy farmland countryside
with a Liberty Bell (albeit cracked,) and a humble, independent feel.

4th – 1788 – GEORGIA

Founded by General James Oglethorpe (though with mixed motivations,
he respected the Indians,) after a charter, 1732
to be a colony for the homeless and prisoners who couldn't pay debts--
GEORGIA from King George 2.

But the first colonists were actually traders and farmers,
and their servants and dear families...
to lands inhabited by Cherokees, Seminoles, and
                    the Creek Confederacy of Tribes
who were not plagued by religious homilies.

Previously, Spanish missions, French traders,
and English colonizers all vied for the Plains,
once inhabited by woodland natives, moundbuilders,
Creeks, Cherokee—all descendants of chiefdoms that reigned.

The colony of Georgia to offset the Spanish
on Florida and Carolina's lands,
but too many crooks spoiled the colonial broth
with power-hungry demands.

And quickly the effects of thousands of years
were reduced by the 'unintentional' European plagues,
and many who once roamed freely
were reduced *intentionally* to English slaves.

The lure of gold drew Hernando de Soto
to north Georgia in the 1540s;
and discovery in early 1800s led to the planned removal
of the Cherokee from *their* territories.

Georgia, known for sun-colored peaches from the Spanish (from China,)
moonlit sweet Vidalia onions, white cotton and peanuts, for starters—
birthplace of Jackie Robinson, Martin Luther King Jr., and President
and Nobel Peace Prize laureate, James (Jimmy) Earl Carter.

10th – 1788 – VIRGINA, and, 35th – 1863 – WEST VIRGINA

He sailed the seas for his dear Queen,
navigator and poet, Sir Walter Ralegh
garnering tea, potatoes, and eventually
he crossed the big lake, jolly.

VIRGINIA in 1584 for Elizabeth,
the "VIRGIN Queen" the trip he did make;
she wasn't married for 60 years—
the land for her name's sake.

You see, she was a "virgin Queen"
they say she palled with nurses,
but who knows what she gave Sir Ralegh
in the form of reimburses.

She played croquet by the river Thames
watching for the Spanish armada,
but as American history goes—
no English child could claim her "muthah" or any man "fadda".

She was 'fair', well-liked, and petite,
wore hoop dresses and white make-up,
secretly financed the plunder of Spanish settlements and ships—
her pseudo-name, a part of history's break-up.

As George had wooden
or were they hippopotamus ivory teeth,
hers were iron, then wooden, then porcelain,
no problem chewin' the beef.

And when the Western Counties of Virginia
refused to secede from the States United,
in 1863 the mountainous region opposing slavery,
WEST VIRGINIA, itself invited.

With miners (of all ages) hardworking,
the earth mined for deposits of coal;
FDR helped establish labor unions
though for many the work took its toll.

Again might the Virgin be proud
of the men laboring under duress,
with fluorescent third-eyes and a blackface-disguise,
overall odds they endure and coalesce.

Though her pride would perhaps diminish
knowing American slavery first started
when Africans were shipped to Jamestown--
from their *homeland* forcibly parted.

And the British loss of Yorktown to the French and 'U.S.'
was the revolutionary war's decisive battle
leading to the 13 colonies. Don't forget:
13 sections on the Turtle's medicine rattle.

And the names and the people live on
with stately grace
reminders of the people
with different faces

who stopped—

and looked—

and named the places....

all landmarks of the human race.

This beauteous place—
the Indians call Turtle Island.
And the lesson remains—you can claim
but you must caretake land!

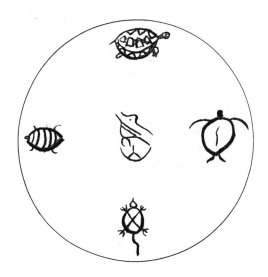

7
OF FRENCH (mostly)

More of a battle between England and France,
1756-63, for colonial excavations,
the French and Indian, or Seven-plus Years' War,
was more of a mini-world-war of nations.

The French were more drawn to trade
while the English sought land as their saviour,
but to those whose home where this commerce perpetrated—
this was *all* very strange behaviour!

The first Treaty of Paris, 1763,
put an end to all that? Not really.
The second Treaty, 1783,
ignored the Indians by glances most steely.

The French gave their lady Liberty
to be statue watching over the harbor,
a support for the growth of personal freedoms
like flower from vine around arbor.

14th – 1791 – VERMONT

Green Mountains perched
above the northeast corridor,
where fur, lumber, syrup and fishing
were once (and still are) a lure.

GREEN MOUNTAIN "Vert(d) Mont",
(probably from explorer Samuel de Champlain's 1677 map)
                                        formed in 1777,
where maple syrup was tapped from Indian skills;
autumn foliage, snowy cabins—a given.

Champlain's historical gunshot killed two Mohawk chiefs
and led to battles and beaver pelts to take,
with the Iroquois siding (sort of) with the Dutch and English,
against the French....and even *still*, named after *him*— a Lake.[113]

Originally of the Wabanaki Confederacy,
Abenaki and bands in various directions,
of Vermont, Maine, New Hampshire, Massachusetts,
    southern Quebec- Canada, New York, Connecticut, and westward—
despite European infections.

Algonquian maple syrup "sinsibuckwud" 'drawn from wood'
from holes in trees where birch bark buckets hang.
Abenaki, "True Men", "Dawn Land People of the East",
watched golden Sunlight bathe the coast—birds sang.

White settlers and traders added metal kettles
and to this day the maple syrup thrives.
Now on pancakes and waffles we can slowly remember....
the origins of a people still alive.

18th – 1812 – LOUISIANA

The first European to descend the Mississippi to the delta,
for fur, French explorer (Robert Cavelier) Sieur de La Salle,
for LOUIS XIV of France, (1682) LA LOUISIANNE
best known for the Mardi Gras ball.

Though a warrior-king, they say he brought peace,
reformed army and administration;
his father passed on when he was a mere boy, so, at age five
(the absolute monarch to be,) little Louie headed the nation.

The man, Louis XIV chose the Sun as his emblem,
both from Indian chiefs, and Apollo, god of peace and the arts;
he had many offspring from royal love affairs
at the court where madames won his hearts.

The path of the sun in his layout of gardens
traced the hours of all of his days,
and he burgeoned French culture with theatre and music,
arts, sciences, and the Royal Academies.

À propos to the French, LOUISIANA's well-known
for spiced cooking both Creole and Cajun,
for gumbo, spicy sauce, jambalaya, and crawfish,
and a French quarter to keep you from aging.

For a hotbed of parties and street dances
to the beat of a musical stew
spiced with jazz, zydeco (blues, tunes French and Caribbean)—
give a tip of the hat to ol' Lou.

But in lieu of Louis XIV...Louis XVI, that's another story
of Bastille, beheadings, and a French Revolution
across the sea...*another* wave of revolting!
(1789-93) — for the bourgeois...retribution.

And another Louis, perhaps truer to this state's name
is good-spirited, trumpet-playing Armstrong,
whose raspy voice and handkerchiefed brow
shine with the trademark bellows of Satchmo's song.

Now Louis' singing should give us some cheer
considering La Salle's expedition,
where he claimed Louisiana for his good king
though never asking the Indians permission.

And the names and the people
live on with grace,
first named from what
they saw or lived nearby,

of Earth
and of the flowing Waters
upon which
the people steered by.

Rides through water
and on land,
Turtle gifts of Perseverance
Here on Turtle Island.

Rides through water,
breathes on land,
Turtle Prayer and Perseverance
Here on Turtle Island.

This beauteous place—
the Red Race call Turtle Island,
and the lesson remains—you can take
but you cannot own land!

And the African-Americans, used as slaves,
when the Indians would no longer suffice,
ALL helped build the fabric of this country
with Whites and Asians and others—each one can give advice.

Respect and befriend all of the races
by at least Understanding if you don't agree,
for each of the races is a reflection of Self
and a part of the wholeness Spiritually, Mentally and Planetarily.

Conquer and befriend your Shadowy-self,
Purify the impurities of your Duality-self,
Activate the fullness of your Whole-self
Attain the perfection of your Highest-self.

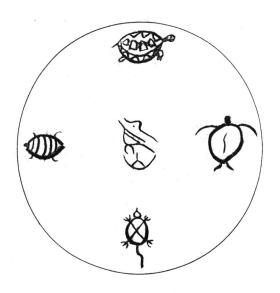

8 - OF DISTICT and ANNEXATION (mostly)

1791 - WASHINGTON D.C.
From lands of Maryland and Virginia
a federal territory was declared
on lands going back to 9000 B.C.
where Piscataway Indians fared.

The DISTRICT OF COLUMBIA or WASHINGTON D.C.
(for COLUMBUS, oh, how fittin',
the 'discoverer' of America)
where history and laws have been easily re-written.

Granted, he was an able adventurer
'cross wind and white-capped ocean,
but greed and slaves from pillaged lands
oft' neglected in history books' devotion.

Seems any hero fits the bill
a peg to toss a hat on,
some name to hoist a flag of fame.....
instead of back to pat on.

A pirate flag once waved on ship,
on land reflects territory,
though skull and bones are traded in
that's not the end of story.

The District of Columbia,
a.k.a. George Washington D.C.—
a much debated Capitol of
WE THE PEOPLE?....WE will see.....

Rides through water,
breathes on land,
Turtle Prayer and Perseverance
Here on Turtle Island.

1898 – ANNEXATIONS
GUAM, an unincorporated territory
given up by Spain in 1898,
and WAKE ISLAND annexed in that same year—
the bounties of the Spanish-American War at the going rate.

PHILIPPINES also under U.S. control
due to the same circumstances,
though Independence gained in 1946[114]
when they must have had *some* island-dances.

1898 – PUERTO RICO

The last on this list
but truly one of the first,
the Taino Indians (also of San Salvador,) Arawak-speaking
with peaceful-ness they quenched their thirst.

Perhaps no full-bloods exist today
yet their culture continues though the blood has thinned,
according to Columbus they were sweet-tongued, laughing,
gentle, muscular and copper-skinned.

The Taino Indians, Taino "good or noble" (people),
friendly and peaceful, farmers and fishermen
gathering together for the singing of *their* village epic—
again and again.

With Columbus, on his second voyage to Haiti,
King Ferdinand of Spain, to the Tainos sent a threatening letter:
'You must bow to our Lord, you barbarians,
or we'll start war...really, it's for the better.'

But what he and many others
have failed to see,
is that there are *many* already bowing to
and embracing— the everlasting, peaceful Tree!

Sweet-tongued, laughing and gentle,
the Arawak-speaking (also people of the Caribbean, Cuba, Haiti,
    Guyana, Surinam, Dominican Republic, Venezuela)
    Taino (on lands now called Cuba, Bahamas, Dominican
    Republic and Haiti (Hispaniola)) Indians—
but the world *they* knew was ending...
as the history of the U.S. America begins.

When Arawak slaves were practically extinct,
the Spanish, avoiding *their* own labor pains
to mine for gold,
shipped Africans instead, in chains.

PUERTO RICO from Spanish "RICH PORT"
with barrios. The beaches are calming.
A self-governing commonwealth in 'union'
with the U.S....abused by Vieques test-bombing.

The Coquí, a much-revered 2 inch tree-frog
sings the nighttime like a bird;
a starlit walk and up in the branches
"ko-KEE ko-KEE" is heard.[115]

9
THE INVASION (mostly)

The Spanish from the South (and West), French from the North—
    from all four of the directions;
the English and Dutch from the East, Russians from the Northwest—
    bringing cultural infections.

Feigning that the Indigenous Peoples had no culture
the Invaders were frothing with polemics,
bogus treaties for land, seeking gold and resources—
but to the wilderness People.....they brought epidemics.

From other places they came,
to a landmass of unfettered ritual;
how would that feel to be 'surrounded', as such,
by the ever-hungry habitual?

Though cultural exchanges also bring teachings
enriching and expanding one's cultural learnings,
when forced and enforced with unwelcome pressures
they subvert peoples' natural yearnings.

10
WHAT ARE YOUR NAMES?

i
While
All the while
The Un-Nameable

the amiable Un-Nameable gives aid,
buoys wind and wave, maps the course
and puts color to sky and cheeks—dear friend.

ii
And what is your real Name? my friend,
the name whispered to you in the quietest of moments,
the name visioned in the darkest of night,
the name felt by you in the deepest of reverence and humility.

And the name shouted across the open field
to bridge the grass and wormy distance between strangers.

What is your true name? my friend,
the name that calls you to a higher calling,
the name that calls you to a humble bowing,
the name God (or whatever you call THAT)
calls you and you are called to loving attention.

iii
And the nick-names, the pet-names,
the playful generics of human camaraderie,
the common name that calls you to action,
the names your friends give you.

The name called to the never-seen-before human-being to befriend,
the name called between long-time friends long-knowing each-other

And the name an enemy once called you
before you called across the open field
to melt the hailed and flaky distance,

While
All the while
The Amiable Un-Nameable

11
OF LAND (CONCEPTS)

To the Indians (and others) land is community,
a sacred part of our being.
To conquerors (and others) a commodity—
two different ways of seeing.

The concept of ownership is
a choice of perception—
to parcel out land, or,
reach out to the four directions.

Much of all history
and the pieces worth telling
revolve around land and its resources—
for the sharing, or taking, or selling.

Native cultures migrated seasonally
adjusting to patterns of weather,
while most explorers chased a carrot
ignoring roadside's grey-pink-purplish-red heather.

There are wide-open spaces
to stir all your senses,
or, for privacy's sake
there are chain-link (and other) fences.

To the Indians, land
is a gift from the Creator,
a global surface whose caring for
is its own liberator.

    And the names and the people
    live on with grace,
    first named from what
    they saw or lived nearby,

    of Earth
    and of the flowing Waters
    upon which
    the people steered by.

    This beauteous place—
    the Red Race call Turtle Island.
    And the lesson remains—you can claim
    but you cannot own land!

OF LAND (VISIONS)

Many tribes across many areas
now neatly shaped as states;
once...vastly different borders,
with vast wide-open gates.

The gradual takeover of indigenous lands
by various peoples from countries approaching,
is best summed up by Tecumseh, a Shawnee:
"...never contented but always encroaching."

Driven from wilderness homelands...to reservations...
to allotted parcels weakening tribal affiliation....
to cultural assimilation...
and attempts at a peoples extermination...

for land, gold, cotton, railroads and ranches,
whatever the item deemed most of need,
for water, livestock, sugar, beets, forests, coal, oil, natural gas,
                                                          uranium—
ALL for relentless greed,

abetted by religions and possessive psychologies,
abusive and scam business practices
of slavery, missions and crusades
with false treaties, false trusts, and false taxes.

With WorldCom, Enron, and insider trading
the "never contented" keep dangling the hook;
while the struggle to care for the homeland continues,
you'd best keep an eye on your pocketbook.

Divide and conquer,
that is the method of war mentality.
Accepting differences, and reaching out with compassion
makes respect and healing a reality.

OF RECORDS

Written records are helpful
as are symbols, patterns, song and story-telling;
truly cultured worlds are circular,
while the strictly linear move like a felon.

Written records are guides
and recorders of essential information,
yet re-cords are cords encoded
for whenever you forget your natural elation.

The oral traditions of stories and teachings
passed down from the elders are essential;
through word-of mouth and un-recorded learnings
run pathways of energy not captured by pen, type, computer or pencil.

12
OF PROPHECY TO PRESENT

And the names live on with stately grace
reminders of those— who still among us!
with amazing foresight prophesied:
before an Age of Flowering—an Age of Rust.

Hence, witness all the rusted vehicles
symbol of a fast-track freedom,
the vacant metal office buildings—
pity, some thought of the Indians: 'we don't need 'em.'

And perhaps by Rust they mean something greater,
like corrosion of the natural ways,
and distancing from harmonious landscapes,
and drifting... in a neon haze,

like large metallic dinosaurs
in an Ice Age of the spiritual ways.
Give birth to worldly remedy,
on Flowering let us fix our gaze!

And just how united
are United States?
Much paperwork and fees
just to change your license plates.

And just how united
are United States?
when a quarter of a half of a whole
can decide (possibly) electoral fates?

Each state like a country
with accents and cultures, and laws that preside,
yet bound by Constitution and Bill of Rights (possibly)
and a free spirit that cannot be denied!

    And the names of the people
    live on with grace,
    first named from what
    they saw or lived nearby,

    of Earth
    and of the flowing Waters
    upon which
    the people steered by.

    This beauteous place—
    the Red Race call Turtle Island
    and the lesson remains—you can buy
    but you cannot own land!

    And the names live on
    with stately grace,
    reminders of the people
    with different faces

    who stopped—

    and looked—

    and named the places.....

    all landmarks of the human races

    all filtering disgraces
    to arrive at an oasis
    transcending the stasis
    on a case by case basis

    been put through the paces
    so the suffering erases
    though a scar remains in places
    reminders of what defaces

to be healed with sweet caresses

      on the bodies and the faces
      until there are no traces
      of any vague malaises
      or *aggressive* army bases

      though a scar remains in places
      reminders of the crisis
      been put through the paces
      no more suffering on the faces

to be healed with sweet caresses

      leaving only spiritual aces
      balancing leather and laces
      covering all the bases
      on a case by case basis

      and the names and the people
      live on with grace,
      first named from what
      they saw or lived nearby

      of Earth
      and of the flowing Waters
      upon which
      the people steered by

        all landmarks of the human races

13

OF HEALING

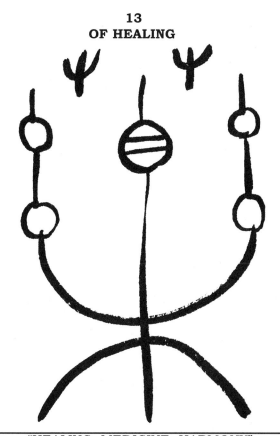

"HEALING; MEDICINE; HARMONY"

a Frame or Tree Ꝛ
with Drum ⊖
Bells o
Sprouts; Herbs; Grass Ψ

The ancient Chinese here reveal that true Healing has to do with restoring Harmony. Music and Happiness are part of Harmony as this pictograph, without the Sprouts, Herbs.. signifies "Music and Joy". The Yellow Emperor's Healing Music is an ancient classic that utilizes musical 'tones' for health and well-being, and is well worth a listen. American Indians consider the Drum to be the "heartbeat" of the earth; and bells, small and large, are used ceremoniously in Tibetan and Asian temples and rituals. The Chinese, American Indians and other tribal peoples know much about the healing properties of natural Herbs. The American Indian's sacred "prayer pipe" and "smudging" ceremonies are also known for encouraging Healing and Harmony. And various Indian peoples refer to wise use of totems from the animal kingdom as "good medicine". The 'Tree' of Life is recognized Universally.

Now perhaps you'll notice
particular cultural flavors:
most Indian names for Nature and Groups of People;
most foreign for Individual names to favor.

All the state names reflect
an ongoing issue to deal with:
natural elements, tribes and clans of Common People
subjugated by the ruling elite—tough to live with.

And not a single mention...................
of a race brought here against *their* will
as slaves. Now called African-Americans,
the lack of recognition—a bitter pill!

What past treatment of the Indians and Indigenous peoples in America;
what the holocaust to the Jews, Gypsies, and Gays;
what the British Empire to the Australian Aboriginal peoples;
                              Stalin to the Russian people:
what anyone depriving *anyone* their own true ways!

OF HEALING (of the 4 RACES)

The healing of the 4 races
is the healing of this nation
(and planet) 4 colors of the circle,
alchemical, and of each station.

Do not be deceived
by mere outward appearance--
improve daily living conditions
with compassionate and devoted adherence.

BLACK-man-song-and-dance, kept in inner cities
portrayed as a shiftless thug
addicted to a 'trafficking' problem
of substances 'pumped in' by the government—drugs!

WHITE-man-guitarist, cruisin' on the highways
fast paced nation feelin' no pain,
numbed... by scenic outlooks
and a drug of choice—cocaine!

RED-man-drummer, kept on reservations
through forced relocation by genocidal conquerors with excess gall,
depriving him full access to nature 'spirits'
and so, replaced by—alcohol!

GOLD-man, dis-Oriented
in World War II, Korea, and Vietnam...
background vocals chanting,
we could learn from him—exquisite calm!

BLACK-woman-singer mama
sister of the night,
Sojourner of truth,
dispels the children's fright.

WHITE-woman homemaker,
feminist, and corporate prostitute,
a core of hidden strengths,
and a skin so smooth as to defy hirsute.

RED-woman-storyteller, herbal, so wise,
so many wrinkles on your face
from sun-baked terrain and with so many children
you share the traditions of this place.

GOLD-woman tea-maker,
wise, compassionate, demure,
you walk along so humbly—
with a glance you re-assure.

BLACK-child with a present
and a future where you stroll,
walk on with grace and pride
your people give this earth soul.

WHITE-child with opportunities
abounding at every turn,
be humble and respectful
and for your people a lesson you will learn.

RED-child you know "we're all related"
from grandmothers and grandfathers you hear it.....
your gift to teach the world
the Nature and Benevolence of Great Spirit.

GOLD-child you see beyond
the limits of here-and-now,
with utmost humility and gracious strength—
you teach the world to bow....

HENCEFORTH

Not too late...
may the United States of America
and/or THE PEOPLE
living on TURTLE ISLAND
dismantle the war-machine,
the military-industrial-etc.-complex,
and turn inward,
and reach outward
with open hands,
open arms
and embrace the African-Americans,
and embrace the White People,
and embrace the American Indians,
and embrace the Asian-Americans,
and embrace all the colors of the rainbow
of skins and minds and spirits.

May the United States of America
and/or THE PEOPLE
living on TURTLE ISLAND
turn inward,
and humbly apologize to the Red Race and to the Land
and give back what there still is to give back
of name,
of place,
of treaty,
of language,
of education,
of respect,
of natural way of life—
and so, stop the habit of conquering
and so, reach out— that we may all proceed from here and now

HENCEFORTH

PART 2
INTER-DEPENDENCE

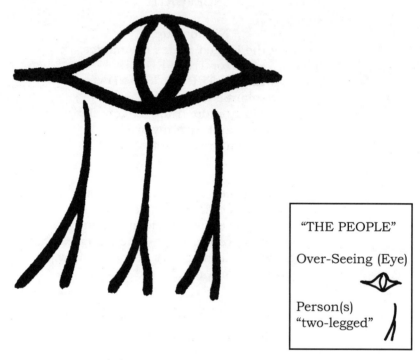

> "THE PEOPLE"
>
> Over-Seeing (Eye)
>
> Person(s)
> "two-legged"

"We hold these truths to be self-evident:
that all human beings, irrespective of race, color, or sex,
are born with the equal right to share at the table of life."

— Emma Goldman, *A New Declaration of Independence* (1909)

1

Mostly from the "Declaration of Independence"
(no need for copyright or permission
because these are *my* words,
these are *your* words,
these are *our* words!):

"We hold these TRUTHS to be *SELF-evident*"
("WE HOLD THESE TRUTHS TO BE SACRED
                            AND UNDENIABLE" - the original draft[116])
"that all Men are created equal"
("THAT ALL MEN ARE CREATED EQUAL AND INDEPENDENT"
    –original)

"All human beings are born free and equal in dignity and rights.
They are endowed with reason and conscience and should act
towards one another in a spirit of brotherhood" (and sisterhood,)
from *Universal Declaration of Human Rights* 1948, Article 1

"that they are endowed by their Creator with certain inalienable
    rights"
("FROM THAT EQUAL CREATION, THEY DERIVE RIGHTS
    INHERENT AND INALIENABLE" – original)
"that among these are LIFE, LIBERTY,
    and the PURSUIT of HAPPINESS—"
freedom to "pursue" so you gotta find it on your own...
"Everyone has the right to life, liberty and security of person."
Universal Declaration of Human Rights, Article 3
and, "uncontrolled enjoyment", that is,
uncontrolled by others, thank you, William Penn!

"that to secure these Rights,
governments are instituted among Men,
deriving their Powers
from the *consent* of the Governed."
"When in the course of human events...
the Laws of Nature and of Nature's God entitle them..."
(this revealing the Benevolence of Nature)

Singing an Epic of Peace:

That all human beings "...are created equal and independent..."
    though some born more spiritually advanced,
that all human beings "...are created equal and independent..."
    though some born more mentally acute,
that all human beings "...are created equal and independent..."
    though some born more physically adept,
that all human beings "...are created equal and independent ..."
    though some born poor or rich,

Yet born equal and independent.
Equal creation inherent
(*thus, already within; thus, NO SUCH THING AS ORIGINAL SIN*)

with Declarations of Inter-Dependence,
Declarations of Human Rights.

To this equal creation,
to this sameness with their Creator,

to this SAMENESS
this EQUAL CREATION

This SPARK of sameness
This SPARK of equal creation

This spark of sameness of equal creation of all men and women,
all birds and animals and fish and crawling ones,
all sentient beings

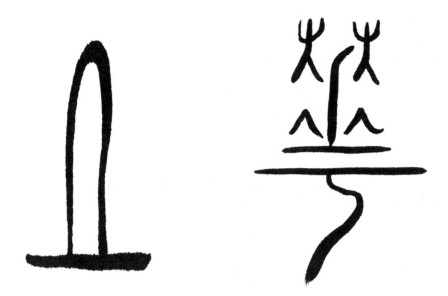

To over-simplify, (and yet give some structure to the whole affair):
the male sexual organ is a "phallic" symbol;
the female sexual organ a "flower". (see p. 31)

Whatever combination of these one partakes of, the symbols are apt, at least to my understanding. The Chinese refer to hetero-sexual activity as "flowery combat", except that 'combat' has a rather different meaning, perhaps equal to the modern phrase "the battle between the sexes", or referring to the 'struggle' during sex. Also, "flowery-combat" has a non-violent interpretation, (although as far as treatment of the whole person, recent U.S. statistics of domestic abuse would prove otherwise.)

Artistically, many of Georgia O'Keefe's beautiful flower paintings have often been compared with the female sexual organ.

And certainly— rockets, missiles, and other such objects are of a phallic symbol nature.

Aside from obvious Freudian connotations, the psychology underlying the use of such lovely 'apparatus' is looked at with the next few poems.

1

How many women have fought for war?
Not many, not many.
Not many women have fought for war,
Not many, not many.

How many men have fought for war?
Too many, too many.
Too many men have fought for war,
Too many, *too* many.

If Men can claim their feminine selves
and ward off war, ward off war.
If Women can claim their masculine selves
and close the door, close the door.

If any can claim their truest selves
and be open for more, open for more:
    Women and Men, two forms
    of the Creator's pour!

2

Singing an Epic of Peace
of the boyfriend
being a: boy   friend

of the girlfriend
being a: girl   friend,
and the lover being a lover.

Many have a preference,
a mode of sexual bliss—
mostly just a choice
of whom and where and when which orifice.

Metaphor: a figure of speech
in which a word or phrase
literally denoting one kind of object or idea

is used in place of another
to suggest a likeness
or analogy between them.

Let's play metaphor,
Let's play comparing images,
Let's play army-soldier
Let's play phallic-symbol.

And so, consider this:
a soldier with his helmet,
the shape looks like this—
a phallus with its rounded, arching head...
Please! Consider this:

How many have died in battle,
from neglecting this—
brothers enjoying eachother's company
(Yes, even with a kiss.)

A kiss feels good,
no one would deny this,
but narrow minds have put a shame on men
so, Please! Consider this:

The kiss has played through Hollywood
as pinnacle of bliss,
between the two sexes
her lips, and his.

A kiss goodbye toward battle
a promise to be strong,
a kiss upon homecoming,
"boy, that movie wasn't *too* long."

Oh, yes, the kiss was welcome,
the kiss felt good, that's for sure,
but consider what a different world
if men touched men instead of war!

Singing an Epic of Peace,
Of the Deity that speaks
From unending hidden crevices
And wide-open gathering places
And from the central pillar
That spirals through us each,

Without cease,
With devoted ease.

Although a touch between brothers
is not the *only* solution,
(why then is this gesture of friendship
so mired in dissolution?)

Because it means *the end of war*
of brother against brother,
and the open celebration
of loving one another.

Singing an Epic of Peace
of the boyfriend
being a: boy   friend,

of the girlfriend
being a: girl   friend,
and the lover being a lover.

A kiss, a touch, one look,
it's all the same,
a sharing of the beauty—
the dying of the shame.

This country founded
on 'brotherly revolution',
now although with many freedoms
still, mired in neglected Constitution.

And so, each must have some (r)evolution
to discover their own mode of bliss,
a personal constitution
of him or hers or this.

Some prefer a marriage;
some, someone of their kind;
some prefer a harem;
some, the solitary climb.

And, real Peace, perhaps is deeper
than all of her or his,
a personal journey
between one's self and Bliss.

And yet, because the sand has lines,
because the trench was dug,
we must keep on singing
of Peace, of Love, of Hugs.

If I fail, sing another song—
If I succeed, sing along,

Singing an Epic of Peace
Beyond the cloak of nations and generations
Before and after the war-torn differences
Of opinions and dominions—
And so, Homage to Thee Within.....

3
Let's play vagina—
Let's play beautiful flower,
Let's play Yoni
Let's play creative and sexual energy,
Let's play lunar-cycle purification—
Let's play the CHOICE is yours.

OR

Let's play vagina,
Let's play creative and sexual energy, womb,
then,
Let's play place for nurturing,
then, giving birth to,
then nurturing,
then setting free:
Let's play...the CHOICE is yours.

Singing an Epic of Peace
of the boyfriend
being a: boy   friend

and the girlfriend
being a: girl   friend

and the lover being a lover.

4
Let's play penis—
the spaceship penis
complete with engine-room testes
still roams the skies
and from up on high
sights ancient Grecian 'herms',
stone phallic road-markers
pointing the way with sheer turn-on,
for whichever way you turn
a better road is that which
turns you on,

a better road is that which
one turns on,
and one good turn-on
deserves a brother.

And from up on high
sighting Hindu Shiva's 'lingams',
phallus totems

projecting upward
from templed enclaves

land of a thousand-plus
positions,
all sizes fits all.

And from on high
Unidentified Fornicating Objects,
displayed and splayed and played and laid

as temple art,
the sacred and the sexual
in uninterrupted ecstasy.

And from on high
sighting the un-married,
the once dog-priests, celibate,

Yes, once ago,
the priests did it

doggie-style.

And querying unto his Master
'Father, I have a confession,'
[then the priest whispers,]
'A sort of fancy for,'
[then whispers more softly,]
'the little boys.'

'You must abide your station, faithfully,'
is Father's reply,
'and not transgress cherubic youth,'

Then, Father whispers back with age-old sigh,
'Regarding love of little boys, my sons.... you see...*my son...*
so do I, so do I.'

And from up on high
spaceship penis,
complete with engine-room testes
sights nuns in life-long love affair
with Master, wedded

to the stained glass,
candle-burning, bricklaid edifice,
all carnal love on layaway,
or so the lay preachers say.

And from up on high
this sampling of the varied places
penis seeks to go—
on the one hand, up high,
and sometimes, sometimes, low.

Singing an Epic of Peace
of the boyfriend
being a: boy   friend

of the girlfriend
being a: girl   friend

and the lover being a lover.

5
Let's play metaphor,
Let's play comparing images,
Let's play gun control,
Let's play "well-regulated militia",
Let's play *heal* the psyche.

If men grabbed wienies
instead of guns
we'd all be a lot better off,

and get on much better,
we'd get it on much better
and 'get off' much better.

If governments sold porn, or sex toys
or musical instruments
instead of weapons,
or provided clean water, housing, basic necessities...

We'd all be better off
getting on much better,
getting it on much better
much better 'getting off'.....

WARNING:
Explicit visual poetic metaphor,
frightening to some, far less
troublesome than the evening news,

possibly to be banned from school reading lists
so read at your own consent,
or check with your parents:

READY NOW ????

Let's SEE a metaphor:
Ejaculating from a longish
tubular fleshy substance
with *much* pleasure,

in the hand,
in the mouth,
in the ear,
in the face,
in the ass.....

instead of shooting off
bullets and missiles,
instead of building prophylactic
space defense systems.

What's a metaphor?
To show where energy can go
when directed in different directions.

Peeling away the layers of judgment,
peeling away the layers of societal primness,
of denial of 'natural pleasures'.

Peeling away the layers of religiosity,
peeling away the layers of battle,
and competition, of mine and yours,

of my land and yours, my nation and yours,
my government funded, government approved
weapon of mass destruction, weapon of boost my economy
and yours, peeling away

until our brothers may walk free,
our sisters walk free,
our children walk free,
our animals walk free,
our birds fly free,
our fish swim free,
our plants grow free,
all sentient beings be free,

our brothers walk free...
        onto the field once used for battle

    (the empty shells of their loneliness,
    the empty shells of bullets and missiles,
    as the only things left for dead)

        and embrace

            Peeling away the layers of illusion,
            and façades
            Until....

                In the center of an onion
                there are no tears!

GLOBALLY ECONOMICAL BALLADS

THE BALLAD OF RATES OF EXCHANGE
Originally cattle,
sheep, camel, then grain,
were stocked and stored
to measure one's gain,

and from Oceans— vast shells
for divination, adornment, and rank,
or simply as money—
back when Ocean was a no-interest bank.

From mollusk to wampum
and cowrie shell,
from watery currents that ebb and flow
the markets once dipped in Oceanic-well.

There was chattel, (that's slaves)
as capital too,
and big corporate quicksand
you could sink your teeth into.

"COWRIE SHELLS"

Now we ship across seas,
and by land, rail and air,
no matter the cost
you can get something there.

But the tides have been traded,
movers buy and they sell
like Pavlovian dogs
to a stock market bell.

So for putting our currencies
once again afloat,
and dispensing with medieval
and feudal moat,

and for honoring labor
and creative notion:
when making transactions,
consider the mollusk, consider the Ocean.

THE BALLAD OF THE SAGGING ECONOMY

7 trillion spent on 'defense'
in these United States,
since 1949:
this does not equate.

Now, you tell me
about the sagging economy;
Please don't—
makes me wanna pee..

51 percent of the 1999
United States budget spent,
toward war. For Life, Liberty, and the Pursuit of Happiness
barely a dent.

Now you tell me
about the sagging economy:
Please don't—
whatta travesty.

Ain't no enemies
but those the United States selected:
protecting the citizens?
or a page of Hollywood directed?

Now, you tell me
about the sagging economy:
Please don't—
makes me wanna wee.

1.2 billion people live
on a 1-2 dollars a day;
many have not yet
received their fair pay.

Now, you tell me
about the sagging economy;
Please don't—
Whatta travesty.

THE BALLAD OF CONSPICUOUS CONSUMPTION

As long as you can afford
and, often and very cheaply,
you're better off than worldly poor—
thank God, your pockets deeply.

Up the status ante
with name brands recognizable,
and ever a manifest destiny eye
on markets far east and horizon-able.

Which way to turn when all is conquered?
To whom to sell when all's been sold?
To outer space an untapped market?
For those whose prime-directive's bank-rolled!

"Congress shall make no law
respecting an establishment of religion,
or prohibiting the free exercise thereof;..."
says our First Amendment – honoring simple pidgin.

But Civil War and then the Cold One
had men question 'faith',
and they hoped the heathen to re-assure
by having mammon saith.

So, with the Coinage Act of 1864
and H.R. 619 in 1955 they mussed—
take a gander at our currencies,
metallic, then paper: "In God We Trust"

Some say this is just a 'motto'
to out-'boom' a war-time-'bust',
but imagine the reactions IF
religious-signs heralded: "In Money We Trust"

Wherefore art thou, separation
of money and state?
Wherefore art thou, separation
of corporation and state?

Earn your way with "right livelihood" said the Buddha,
and don't let the 'System' choke you with a collar;
as Gov. Jesse Ventura said: "Life's too short
to chase the almighty dollar."

As said by President Jimmy Carter (July15, 1979, speech):
a country that "worships self-indulgence and consumption"
                                                    has gone amiss,
when..."human identity" becomes defined "by what one owns",
and not "by what one does" or, who one IS.

THAT potential turning point for America
affected Carter's popularity,
and led to the Hollywood election
and other trickle-down hilarity.

> Divine energy exists within
> the life of *every* thing,
> IF spirited energy in the making of something
> each little creator puts in.

PART 3

CULTURAL, HISTORICAL, & ETYMOLOGICAL BALLADS

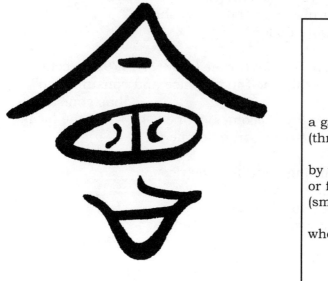

"SOCIETY;
GATHERING;
MEETING;
ASSEMBLY"

a gathering
(three or more)

by the door;
or fireside
(smoke outlet)

where people speak

(words from mouth)

1
Let's play metaphor,
Let's play wean the kiddies
Let's be aware of golden arches
shaped like tits.

Let's be aware of Boob-tube culture
fed on fast food,
fed up with

Hollywood-movie-ad-package-ad-nauseam-meal-deal-next-to-
nothing-costs-huge-budget-product-association-product-
recognition-Military-Industrial-(government-corporate-media-
banking-insurance-stock market-E.P.A.-SupremeCourt-judicial-
oligarchic-etc.
Complex (thank you Dwight D. Eisenhower, so simple.)

Fed up with 'fast food' oxymoron,
'consumer confidence' oxymoron,
'compassionate conservative' oxymoron
'professional sports a game' oxymoron,
'industrial park' oxymoron,
'state-of-the-Art' oxymoron,
'free press' oxymoron,

"...deriving their Powers from the Consent of the Governed"
   oxymoron,
'peacekeeper missile' oxymoron,
'friendly fire' oxymoron, ('hostile fire' redundancy,)
'holy war' oxymoron,
'politically correct' oxymoron,
'pre-emptive self-defense' oxymoron,
'virtual reality' oxymoron.

And Prozac sit-calm,
Primetime sit-com,

Legally drugged youth
and adults...
'Illegally' drugged ('legal'—grown from the earth of its own accord
         "the Laws of Nature and of Nature's God entitle them")
weed, ("self-evident"),
'illegally' imprisoned concentration-camp citizens.

Anyone imprisoned
for eating dandelions? (also a weed),
sautéing mushrooms? (also grown from the ground),
peeling onions? ("...created equal and independent...")

Let's be aware of
Democracy as a mask for Global Capitalism.

Let's be aware of planned obsolescence and
unplanned parenthood.

Let's be aware of potentially
Economic Totalitarianism;
already Cultural Imperialism.

Let's wean the kiddies,
wean the culture
from "fruitful and multiply"
mega-corporate
at the expense of quality-control,
free-choice,
and consumer well-being
CULTURE

2
THE BALLAD OF PROPAGANDA

Congregation de propaganda fide
established by Pope Gregory XV in 1622-23;
(also a "college" Pope Urban VIII). *Propaganda*: "in order to injure
                    an opposing institution, cause or person".
Witness how a policy of no-birth control and only sanctioned
                marriages has affected the population AND the psyche:

'To propagate the species' selected info. is chosen
with disregard for the TRUE story;
regard these words with care,
lest YOU become just another subjugated missionary territory.

What is propaganda?
From the word propagate:
'of plants' - to breed from parent stock;
'ideas' - to disseminate.

So, propaganda's aim
is *fucking* with your mind:
'stay away from any strangers—
simply mate, and true love you'll find.'

The species has been fruitful, and certainly multiplied,
but this trend we'd better sloweth,
or else over-crowding will devour us
that's why (except in rare cases) I'm for Zero-Population-Groweth!

Religions, governments and advertisements
propagate messages of 'cradle to grave',
a means to hook the 'customer'
into being a good-citizen-slave.

These powers love to multiply
more and more the babies they can rear,
to feed their militaristic fantasies
of domination by fear.

These powers love to multiply
more and more the 'products' they can sell.
Honest business has its place: but BEFORE you buy their rap—
ASK— for WHOM tolls the bell?
....WHOM tolls the bell?
....tolls the bell?
....the bell?
....bell?

3

THE BALLAD OF FREEDOMS OF SPEECH & NO-SPEECH

"Are you now
or have you ever been..."
blacklisted, or a member
of the Hollywood Ten?

This question posed
to artists suspect,
of Communist philosophies,
some, then unable to ever direct.

Some would not answer
pleading the Fifth,
others, tattle-tailing
on their kith.

Create what you love
from your personal bent,
just don't speak out
against the government.

That's what McCarthyism
and the House on Un-American Activities
were saying with stagnant hate,
attempting to control—
Art, and church, and state.

The artistic Gestapo
said, 'tell on your friends,
for all your free thinking
this will make amends.'

Yet some stood firm
they knew their true worth
crossed cultural barriers—
the salts of the earth.[117]

So, don't take for granted
the words from your mouth;
because some refused to answer—
you carry your freedoms, west, north, east, and south!

4

THE BALLAD OF WATERGATE

If one could say the turning points
of this young country's fate,
'twould be the loss of JFK,
Vietnam, and the burglary of Watergate.

Back when hungry reporters
could freely investigate,
uncovering a stash of covert deception
at the hotel Watergate.

Deep Throat said, 'follow the money',
money often is the bait,
toward ego, election, and control,
and a belly of power to sate.

If one could say the turning points
of We The People's faith,
(after the Indians) 'twould be the loss of JFK,
Vietnam, and the Watergate wraith.

Nixon swore on a bible, on the Constitution,
on a winter's day—but where were the black-billed rooks?
'Twere Woodward and Bernstein type-tapping
though the Prez assured "I am not a crook".

Also then, was the birth of a phrase
showing skills deemed the most evasive,
a 'non-denial denial',
like 'no comment', so unpersuasive.

The entire U.S. intelligence community
had to self-examine with a clean slate:
the FBI, CIA, Department of Justice—
all because of Watergate.

Now a man bear's the right to privacy
in the comfort of his home or hotel,
and the way to a fair election
is to vote—not to snoop, nor to smear, nor to sell.[118]

5
THE BALLAD OF THE MERCHANTS OF VENEER

The AD pays for the broadcast show,
the PRODUCT is the lord to woo—
but deeper than the THING itself
is the MESSAGE and its mental coup.

Watch the colors on the screen,
see the people smilin' new,
buffed and polished, brash and trim,
dis-proportionate to demographics true.

Drink a foam, and meet some babes,
make a trade...just name your GOO,
defy your age, but do it now
in the ever-polished milieu.

FILTER the noise on broadcast show,
the sponsor is the lord to woo—
of TV, mag., and even
ancient radioo-oo-oo.

Give me facts, (that's all I need)
of what the product can and cannot do,
not some slick creative pitch
they want my fantasy to imbue.

Sex sells, of course, and heck, why not,
the oldest known profession—
but please step aside you middlemen-pimps
if you give no guarantee of undressin'.

Some graphics nice and humor too,
I'll give 'em that, for all their impressin';
but when the CONTENT of the show's a SLAVE—
can't buy the false confessin'.

6

THE BALLAD OF THE SCREEN PULPIT

Bemoan the celebrated blood and gore
on movie and TV,
and recognize its antecedent—
Judeo-Christianity,

which put its hero on a cross
and thorns inside His head,
a seemingly forever box-office-hit—
Him, hanging there for dead.

They put their hero on a cross,
and left Him there for dead.

Much better to see Him play
upon the desert sands,
or laughing with his open-heart
with bread and wine in open hands!

More fitting, see Him in yourself
bathed with light and loving clarity,
not tolerating selfish bullshit—
yet, guiding deepest love...with alacrity.

And, Stop wailing by the wailing wall
and banging on your heads,
much better, put a mirror there—
Look!....at your*selves* instead!

Most folks agree there is One God
but each thinks that *they've* got 'em,
and some say, there are gods within us each—
from shining top to sacred bottom,
(and back to shining top!)

Look!....at your god-selves instead,
from shining top to sacred bottom,
(and back to shining top!)

Bemoan the celebrated blood and gore
on movie and TV,
and recognize its antecedent—
sacrificial idolatry,

which placed some living being
on a sacred altar,
to appease a spiteful so-called-god,
and lead men to slaughter.

Much better to see One play
upon the desert sands,
or laughing with open-heart,
with meat and drink in open hands!

More fitting, see One in yourself
bathed with light and loving clarity,
not tolerating selfish bullshit—
yet, guiding deepest love...with alacrity.

Most folks agree there is One God
but each thinks that *they've* got 'em,
and some say, there are gods within us each—
from shining top to sacred bottom,
(and back to shining top!)

Look!....at your god*selves* instead,
from shining top to sacred bottom,
(and back to shining top!)

7
THE BALLAD OF ART AND PORNOGRAPHY

All pathologies aside,
(any fetishes are yours to deal with,)
let's explore pornography—
and the pleasures *that* pleasure gives.

Have sex with a lover
which no one can see;
videotape that, and show to a friend,
now it's called...pornography!

Remember the artists
who made naked art
now shown in museums and art classes
...'twas pornography's first start.

Breasts have had their fair shake,
the cleavage revered in this:
famous art work, commercial ads,
a hint of marital bliss.

But lo, whatta monopoly
against private parts, vagina and penis,
rarely ever witnessed
except as pornographic, and so, consider this—

How is *that* 'pornographic'?...
when EACH has one of this,
mostly just a choice
of breasts and vagina, or penis.

Is 'pornographic' nakedness?
Or the taking off of clothes?
Or simply what is made for public viewing
in a room judged to be closed?

Woman's and Man's
basic desires the same,
only the sophistication
of the medium has changed.

For which came first,
the Art, or the Body and all *that* holds dear?
and, is the Body, the Art, the Medium,
or the Viewing what is feared?

According to the dicktionary
what you're now reading is 'graphy' of 'porno',
from the Greek "graphein" 'to write'; _
'prostitute or harlot' from Greek "porne"

"...intended to cause sexual excitement...",
a balm to the forlorn;
for some, simple minded pleasures,
or a techno-prostitute called 'porn'.

8
THE BALLAD OF TECHNOLOGY

(Greek: tekhnologia "systematic treatment of an art or craft"

tekhne "art, craft, skill" + -logia, -logy, logos:
"reason, science, study, theory, word, speech")

To manage the accelerating pace
of hardware's rapid data,
stay aware of art and craft
brought forth from "Deus Ex Machina".

The tools are only as beneficent as
'the God out of the Machine';
the colorful flower blooms outward
on stalks so long and green.

Who could craft the stripes on tigers,
and art of butterflies,
but One whose hardware-software program
in the face of logic flies.

Though to *that* One perhaps logical
in a time-lapse sort of way,
as seeds bear the patterns of flower and fruit,
and night gives way to day.

Having woven a structure to house the soul,
a vehicle of body-mind-spirit—
The Creator hooked up all the chips...
within reach of those who don't fear it.

9
THE BALLAD OF OPINIONS & NO OPINIONS

Through education, media blitz, and ad campaigns
the way the many have been shaped by the few.
How much of what you think comes from your *true* self?
Look inside your mind: does all THAT rule you?

The way to manufacture an opinion[119]
is extremely crafty indeed,
'they' appeal to your unrequited childhood senses
and tap you where you *need*.

Or, with convincing false research to back a pre-determined point
an authoritative statement with a tag line is made.
So goes the promotion of a fed.-med.-edu.-peddler
to convince you of a lifestyle to make the grade.

False opinions are subtly shaped
by confusing the part for the whole,
but for gods' sake...don't take my word for it:
look, listen, & explore what you're told!

BLACK RACE
Throughout history the appeal of religions
a way to say we are nothing but dust,
and though some truths embedded in such institutions
Witness the bravery—
        of one, Rosa Parks, who refused to move,
                                on a Montgomery, Alabama bus.

Throughout history the appeal of warfare
a way for the twisted to experience glee,
and though much valor displayed by soldiers
Witness the bravery—
        of one, who voted against undisputed war, on Sept. 14, 2001,
                        Rep. California, Barbara Jackson Lee.

WHITE
Throughout history the appeal of governments,
a way for the few, power over the masses to gain,
and though some security in such institutions
Witness the bravery—
    of one, whose radical views cost him his popularity,
        True-Revolutionary, free-thinking Thomas Paine.

Throughout history the shackles of repression
a way for the fearful, the citizens to mold,
and though some protection with pieces of legislation
Witness the bravery—
    of the sole dissenter of the Patriot Act, on Oct. 11, 2002,
        Wisconsin Senator, Russ Feingold.

RED
Throughout history the taking of land
a way for the spiritually empty to feel full,
and though some fruits of labor extracted
Witness the bravery—
    of one, (and his tribe) who refused to move,
  Sioux Indian, Tatanka Iyotake (Tatanka-Iyotanka), Sitting Bull.

GOLD
Throughout history the appeal of might to mask fear
a way to sway a mass of men,
and though strength embedded in such behavior
Witness the bravery—
    of one, who refused to move from in front of an army tank,
    in "The Square of the Gate of Heavenly Peace" –
        Tian'anmén

10
VOW OF THE GATE OF HEAVENLY PEACE ON EARTH

To face
and face down
that raging strength of destruction,
that violent capability
within yourself,

and pledge to channel
any violent, harmful, or injurious energy,
any violent, harmful, or injurious thoughts,
any violent, harmful, or injurious emotions
anytime they arise,

....into a Peaceful way,
....a constructive way,
....a Radiant Illumination way,
....a Fifth World way,
....a Benevolent way

To pledge never to use violent means,
except, except (by some)
in justifiable, praying for the enemy, life-saving self-defense.

**Until you have made
such a vow....
READ NO FURTHER!**

BOOK 3
HEROES, GODS, AND MOUSAI (MUSES)

"The hero is commonly the simplest and obscurest of men."

-- Henry David Thoreau

"CH'I"
the vital force of energy;
breath; spirit.

The Sun ☉
connected to
Fire 火
&
the overall suggestion
of a Bird (Air) and thus
the Spirit...
attempt to portray this
'invisible' life-force.

i

M y heroes are the little birds who sing.....
and play amongst themselves, and settle on
a sacred branch to drink the sunlight
to their feathered frames. They drink and eat

and traverse through the billowed air. Upon
such currents we compare to feathered light,
our thoughts and spirits travel through the night;
by day we carry low this heightened height.

ii

Perhaps deep down what was already known
when the fanatics threw away their aerial bones,
and set the world ablaze with even more fanatical power,
striking the military and financial towers.

Though symbol does not stop the grieving,
that was the day we stopped our teething.
Despicable? Preventable?
Just another in a series of fanatical?

Perhaps deep down what was already known
when the fanatics threw away their aerial bones,
the heroes are the common folk,
the heroes are the common folk.

A blind man with his seeing-eye dog
walked down the stairs, he felt the tug
of someone's power
and found safe ground beyond the towers.

All through the smoke and ashen rubble
the still, small voice transcending troubles
seemed to whisper 'priorities'
amidst humble offerings and eulogies,

and searching through Egyptian mythology
perhaps there is some cosmic apology:
the bird, the phoenix consumed itself by fire,
then rose from the ashes of its own pyre.

The bird, the soul that rises higher,
above the test of cleansing fire:
the heroes are the common folk,
the heroes are the common folk.

WE WERE NAKED ONCE

Peeling back the garments
of the past,
we find our bodies chiseled
unabashed.

We were naked once
in marble,
standing

In the raw
with some delighted sculptor
hand-carving our behinds

shaping our private parts—
of gods and goddesses, no less:
Apollo, Hermes, Venus, Dionysus.

And still standing
in museum halls,
chilled to the marble bone,
we look on

comment on the craft,
the style, the grace
yet, never say

"Look! They're naked!"
and even though it's stone...
they *posed* that way

somewhere, *somewhere*
inside the sculptor's
loving mind.

We were naked once
in baths
in ancient Greece
where green ideas

sent ripples
through the course
of humankind,

still dipping
in nude resorts, where mass
of flesh reveals—

there's more to skin and bones
than meets the eye.

We were naked once
born with naked flesh,
awkwardly walking across the beach
into tender hands.

INTRODUCTION TO THE MUSES

What offspring springs off Olympian height
to shepherd our taste, touch, hear, smell and sight?

Fair Zeus, begatter of sparks on earth,
with Mnemosyne, (after the battle of Titans,)
                              mother of multiple births.

She, the daughter of Heaven and Earth,
Uranus and Gaia, of cosmic girth.

Mnemosyne: memory, mindful, assisting recall,
the golden-haired goddess reminds us if we appall.

Fair Zeus, Hey-Seuss, Jesus, Yes-us... the savior,
benevolent, thunderbird behavior.

Nine Muses born from god and goddess
assist mankind with arts and sciences. How odd is

this, we must be prodded to feel;
defy logic to keep an even keel.

Their sheer presences and grace quell strife,
keeping the peace, improving life.

Herein, meet the sacred Muses. Attend-O!
sometimes subtle their innuendo,

and sometimes blatant. *They*, you will meet:
invoke, befriend, embrace their heat.

Nine helpers recorded from ancient Greece
and some quite personal...if you please....

    Oh, and remember:
Memory far more than of the mind—
sense-memory *knows* without much thinking;
and center of memory's ingrained form
is not by rote, but by *heart*...all muses linking.

ancient

"MUSIC; JOY; HAPPINESS"
frame; drum; bells (see p.139)

this
modern
version
projects
these very
qualities

182

THE BALLAD OF THE MUSES

When the MOOSE grabs ya,
Ya gotta go with him!

When the MUSE grabs ya,
You have to listen with her!

i
Build a quiet place inside yourself
where you may Hear the MUSES....
and with their fair suggestions
a friendship you may fuse.

She may whisper in your inner ear
until her song is sung,
or perhaps, like an impassioned lover
moistly thrust her tongue.

They may whisper in your inner ear
and tell you you're well-hung,
but not until you spread the word,
not until *their* song is sung.

They may whisper in your inner ear
like unto Sappho, Greece's fair lesbian;
they're non-denominational,
be you hermit or public thespian.

They may sing so quietly
you'll barely know they're present,
until they hear you softly humming,
dancing...feeling pleasant.

ii
...But when the MOOSE grabs ya...
you'll be rustled about like a rodeo rider
holdin' on for your dear sanity,
kickin' up dirt, prayin' through your shirt,
and gladly forsaking your vanity.

When the MOOSE grabs ya—
you'll be going along for the ride,
wrestlin' with your true feelings and your artistic bent,
until the MOOSE is satisfied.

Amuse, a museum,
a rumination-- muse,
or Sufi Rumi-nation,

a whirl, a swirl,
inspired curl,
creative gestation.

Confused?
Bemused?
Be Mused!

Listen to the Music
sprout!!!!!
your sweet elation!

184

THE NINE MOUSAI (MUSES) FROM ANICIENT GREECE
(Greek: "mousa"; "musa"; plural "mousai")

Before the Nine Muses,
the Elder Three strong—
MELETE: Meditation, or Practice of an Art
MNEME: Memory
AEODE : Song

At Delphi
another three to represent the lyre's strings:
NETE,
MESE,
HYPATE,
all tones a lyre brings.

Mythology's lyre crafted from a Tortoise shell
with strings stretched over the empty back,
creating sounds of earthly song—
some taut, some slack.

May songs of Turtle Island sing
from harmony of many strings,
from metal, wood, water, fire and earth,
and the colors and voices that each race brings.

Various other Muses
of assorted names,

though eventually The Nine—
herein meet their kind.

CALLIOPE
(Greek: kallos "beauty" + ops "voice"
 -- Muse of Epic Poetry)

KALLIOPE the BEAUTIFULLY-VOICED
a hummingbird, an instrument toned
of steam whistles, and played upon a keyboard,
whistling with ELOQUENCE, listening...

a hovering joy, rapid wing-beat
partaking of the nectar poured,
a hero's whistle for those who soar,
an EPIC of spoke and unspoken lore.

She seen with WRITING or WAX TABLET
recording of the longest tales,
considered head of all the Muses
though of one mind behind the veils.

Considered head of all the Muses,
how else record the longest, detailed tales?
Kallos, "Beauty", through various pathways sails:

Calligraphy, the beautiful-lettering;
calliopsis, the beautiful flower;
callipygian, the beautiful buttocks.
Beauty thus, in whatever is beholden.

Orpheus, son of KALLIOPE
(by Apollo, or Oeagrus, a King of Thrace,)
the music from his lyre so magical—
wild beasts mellowed, trees danced, rivers calmed their pace.

What son are you, or what fair daughter?
Your Beautiful-Voice flows like water!

CLIO

(Gk: Kleio, kleiein "to tell, praise, celebrate"
-- Muse of History)

KLEIO, a sea-nymph sister, her heart
upon the waters threw, to test the love
of every sailor: sail your course, or, make
me lover; swim with me upon the sea,
or, make me sister of your HISTORY.

She PROCLAIMER of the SCROLL of deeds
of fame and of the infamous,
her laurel wreath and harbor on that narrow stretch of land
between extremes—the isthmus.

Boreal Clio, zoologically,
a gelatinous, without a shell,
food for whales, the RECORD-KEEPERS tell.
Kleio speaks, yet also listens well.

Eighty-fourth asteroid. Objectively recording history,
yet leaning toward-- respect for highest actions,
with PRAISE and laurel wreath for those of self-less deeds;
her unbiased facts transcending factions.

MELPOMENE

(Gk: "songstress, singer" - from melpein "to sing"
-- Muse of Tragedy.

Gk: Tragedy tragoidia: "goat song" from
                         tragos "goat" + aoide, oide "song"

Comedy komoidia: komos "revel" +"song")

To transcend the path of TRAGEDY
get past the dualism of Comedy.

True life revels and true humor revels life.
Comedies of laughter we applaud
with bellied and facial vibrato.

Something tragic we bemoan,
yet rise above extenuated bravado,
by noting the portrayed
Tragic-Comic whole
as:
LIFE'S LESSONS TOLD
by MELPOMENE, SINGER of TOUGH ODES
and GOAT SONGS.

The goat, denied his horny pleasures:
that's! a tragedy.

Goat-men battling for nymphs:
that's! a tragedy.

Frenzy, mania, 'mental agitation', inflammation of the brain,
delirium, detached from nature,
repression of orgiastic spirituality:
that's! a tragedy.

Dionysus denied his wine:
that's! a tragedy.

The primitive mind, reactionary,
reclusive habits, avoiding social interaction:
that's! criminal.

MELPOMENE, friend to Kokopelli, friend to Pan,
the horny ones
sing your goat-songs,
your moon-howling,

your tough odes
purging us (as Aristotle sang) of "pity and fear,"
giving tragedy the boot,

and bid us receive the light
so we may transcend personal tragedy,
derisive comedy,

thus, dispelling the two-faced
from our true face

and so become
a boon to those befriended and beloved,
unraveling the tangled web we wove,

so we may romp through woods again,
drink wine and greet the long lost friend,
get over the hump and hump again,
drink wine and hump the long lost friend,
so we may romp through worlds again,
drink wine embrace the animal-human-divine friend

find joy with sweat and revelry,
and orgiastic spirituality!

EUTERPĒ

(Gk: euterpēs
eu- "good, well, true" + terpein "to delight, please"
[see Terpsikhore]
-- Muse of Lyric Poetry and Music)

EUTERPE, GIVER of PLEASURE, of MUSIC atmospheric,
you-chirp-ee a songster, bird-like LYRIC;
genus of palms, twenty-seventh asteroid,
and flower garland crowned.

Often seen with double-flute
a doubled joy, re-joy-sing hoot
with lyre cheerful and delight with lute,
and flower-garland crowned.

Lyrics and music intertwined
allied to one creative place,
uplifting for the human race.

Lyric poetry with sounds words make
like wind through holes of empty flute,
accentuated with lyre or lute,

Her pleasured chords
exciting some to Dionysian rite,
and other pleasures within one's sight.

ERATO

(Gk: Erato, erasthai "to love"
-- Muse of Lyric and Love Poetry, and Mime)

What words could match ERATO's LOVE touch?

Beyond the mind
with LYRIC MIME
the farce of foreplay,

the before and after laughter
of sex and cigarette—
but never during!

Beyond the mind—
with dance of Love-MIME
unbridled passion whinnies

with a love as such

only a spirit
entwined with flesh
could give as much.

ERATO crowned with myrtle and roses,

her fingers stroking the lovely lyre
inspiring erotic fires
where fleshy parts do wrestle and gyre
where love is often wine-inspired

all senses to ecstatic crescendo...
the mere
sight of you

skin
sweaty smell
of you

lips
wet-tongue taste
of you

firm
soft-strong touch
of you....

sounds Ooooohhhhhhhhh!!!!!!!

TERPSICHORE

(Gk: Terpsikhore, feminine of terpsikhoros "dance-loving",
    terpein "to delight" + khoros "dance, dramatic chorus" -
    with perhaps a special 'enclosure' for dance)
    --Muse of Dance)

Not mere observer—
full-participant
with one-ness
to the movements
of life:
a wedding of the self
akin to husband and wife.

Or with two
(or more)
upon the floor
DANCE-ENJOYING
in ever-flowing unison
sans strife.

Or even more,
assembled
as DRAMATIC CHORUS
'to delight'
with lyre, choral sing-song soar us

while undulating fleshy grace
displays
the physical body-whore
as partner

of the dancer-spirit, lyre playing,
flower garland TERPSIKHORE,
also choral commentator

"O body swayed to music, O brightening glance,
How can we know the dancer from the dance?"[120]

WHIRLING TERPSIKHORE!

URANIA

(Latin Ūrania, Greek Ourānia, ouranos "heaven"
-- Muse of Astrology, Astronomy and the Heavens)

What can be seen and felt from such a heavenly view?
Perhaps less personal, yet as true:

celestial source of inspiration wheeling from the stars
and spheres permits a timely influence often sought in bars.
OURANIA with scope and breadth beyond the intellectual:
to ASTROLOGY, CELESTIAL THEMES,
                          and affinity with HOMOSEXUAL.

Pointing to CELESTIAL GLOBE
with her STAFF, a metaphysical probe
enCOMPASSing the temporal lobes

lifting souls to higher realms,
transcending that which overwhelms.

What moves some to rape the land,
forsake the realms of Heavenly One?
Loads of Uranium under Turtle's southwest reservations:
remember 'As above, so below', reliable rule of thumb.

Ouranian 'heavenly, upper regions',
an overview perceived beyond military legions.
Urano "roof of the mouth"[121,] Upper palate --
suggestion: place the tip of the tongue there...to connect with
inner ballad,

and through patient meditative-silence hear
with ecstatic receiver, The Music of the Spheres—
the sounds and light of heavenly strings
and all the blessings the ethereal brings!

THALIA

(Gk: thallo-, thall- "young, green shoot", thallos, thallus:
thallein "to sprout"; thaleia "blooming"
-- Muse of Comedy and the Idyllic)

LUXURIANT-BLOOMING, THALEIA
of COMEDY and the IDYLLIC,
present and pastoral, and bucolic,
of plants and flowers a winsome tonic.

Directions quested with rural pursuits
are answered along her wooded routes.
What good cheer spreads in meadowed hours?
Have you never chat with the tall sunflowers?

Amuse! Patroness of festive meetings,
one of the three Graces greetings
bestowing verdant beauty and charm
on road less traveled or frequented farm.

All plant-life asks for
besides sun, soil, air and water bringing,
are the idyllic strains of music
and human voices singing.

FLOURISHING language and longevity
as light as unfurling ivy up a garden wall;
the curves of greenery akin to THALEIA'S
SHEPHERD'S STAFF of guidance tall.

Aristotle's *Poetics* sing
that comedy from "phallic song" was born;
(but please) don't panic— think Pan, and hair, and horns:
you see, the phallus is a growing thing.

Wild herbs and mushrooms give woodland charm
though sometimes rough She means no harm,
let THALEIA spark your wild desire
tamed with laughter near blooming briar.

POLYHYMNIA

(also Polyymnia or Polymnia.
Gk: poly-, from polu-, polus " much, many" +
Gk: humnos, hymnos "song of praise"
Latin: hymnus, Old French: ymne,
Middle English: imne - "hymn"
-- Muse of Sacred Poetry)

POLYYMNIA for the singer and the song,
ORATORY and SACRED for the strong.
Her hymns transcend the him, the her, the void.

Appearing with a thoughtful look,
let pen give sound to storytelling-book,
from deepest thought her hymns are born,
from many books the pages torn.

Pearl or flower crowned
sometimes among the masses found,
the muse of rhetoric
when simple hymns won't do the trick.

Yet, the truest, sacred poems you write
to yourself, your twin, by candlelight,
and sung to the spirits to make you whole,
the songs vibrating through your soul.

MANY SONGS OF PRAISES and multiple hummings
to reap the sounds of her rewards
and hear the rapture of those chords.

THE TENTH MUSE

A Muse of INSPIRATION added,
(though inspiration plays through all,)
attributed to Sappho of Lesbos, (hence Lesbian,)
and lineage of literary women who heed the call.

Perhaps the Tenth, one's personal Muse,
when one has honored all the Nine—
a fusing of their heartfelt forces
poured out as inspiration's wine!

THE ART OF LIFE

The Muses not only for Creative Arts
but for the Art of Life. To be so inspired,
call upon their heartfelt guidance
whenever you question, or, are simply tired.

BOOK 4
HIGHER SELVES: A SAMPLING

"HEAVENLY BLESSINGS;
FORTUITOUS; PROSPERITY"

from Heaven   Under One's Roof

Emanations   the Products

     of the Field

&
living harmoniously with
the four directions

$\mathcal{N}$URSERY RHYMES - TWO

1

QUESTIONS TO ANSWER

Do you sing for your staff?
Do you laugh for your King?
Do you preen for your Maker?
Awaken for your Queen?

Do you talk to your Lord?
Are you moored to the walk?
Do you listen for your Lady?
Shady are you? Or do you glisten?

Did you grow up and party?
Are you arty or a foe?
Do you care for others?
Brothers and sisters are you fair?

Do you pray for your fellow human?
Do you stand for the Way?
Do you rise above your littleness?
Bliss shines through *your* eyes!

2

"AND A LITTLE CHILD..."

Could he, would he
walk on water?
Could he, would he
walk on land?

Did he, bid he
walk on water?
Did he, bid he
walk on land?

Kristos, Kristos
walks on water,
the Lord within
extends a hand.

Even if not physically
upon the fluids he did not stride,
each step upon the pathway ripples
the water flowing far and wide.

Each step upon the pathway ripples,
tread lightly lest you make a wave
for in the end you see, my friend,
it's your own soul that's yours to save.

Each step upon the pathway ripples
and sometimes waves awaken best,
sending us to higher ground
by riding high upon the crest.

No proof of His fair days on Earth;
No proof His shadow on a shroud;
No proof His hanging on a cross;
But it does not matter...inside the Heart His realm is sewed.

Could he, would he
walk on water?
Could he, would he
walk on land?

Yeshua, Yes-us, Jesus, Yeah-Seuss, Hey-Zeus! begatter
of sparks and blessings upon this earth,
Kristos, Kristos,
deity of re-Birth.

Con Doctor Kristos
en el corazón.....
todas las mujeres y los hombres
son salud y listo!

With Doctor Kristos
in the heart.....
all the women and men
are healthy and ready!

    White-Man example of the path
    He purifies the heart of doubt,
    White-Man example of the truth
    transcending labels—what *He's* all about.

OF GILGAMESH: First Recorded Epic

To be pained by loss
and yet move on.

To leave the world of fray
yet return to mend

like Gilgamesh, to turn and toss,
and yet reach out with open palm,

though not over-extend one's stay:
is to find within—the Immortal Friend.

FOR YOU – TREE OF LIFE

You attached the mountain to the ground,
trickled down grains of sand.
You pushed the ocean to sound,
making me glad....to hear feet on land.

You put the music in my bones
holding the fabric together.
You push the song through my loins
making us face one another.

You put the flask to the hip,
god-speed over land, air, and sea.
You put the wit in the quip,
drawing us farther from me.

You put the word on the tongue,
truth, making me speak.
You put the twin within one
achieving triumphant peak.

You put the heart at the center
opened the path with a key.
You make me ache 'til we enter,
stinging my eyes 'til we see.

You put the heart at the center
pushing us farther from me.
You make me shake 'til we enter
teaching me how to BE.

You burn away dross
and safely draw the sword,
on my various self-definitions of loss
and all the useless things that I hoard.

You make me laugh unexpected
and the little-guy always attend,
and wine me through meadows connected.
You! The exactness of friend!

You cross me over the bridge
though the edge one must walk all alone—
until 'land' and the sight of next ridge
where you lovingly make me your own.

Your strength, humbly inherent in all,
Understanding you've been here before
through cycles you contain the traversing,
from your Cup only blessings do pour.

We chant you and circle the space,
Simply-Knowing, and Wise beyond years.
We fly with the wind on our face,
only Light from our song appears.

At the top over-seeing the fog,
Prime-Mover You started the Dance,
putting us all into motion
to learn the secrets of Spirit-romance!

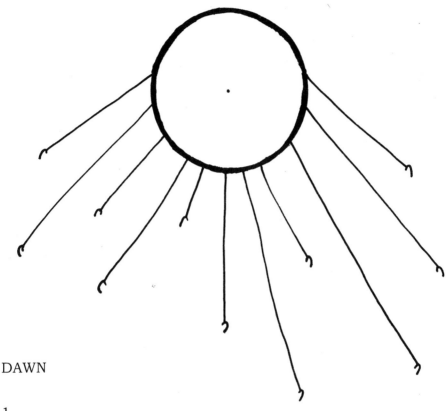

Ancient Egyptian symbol of the SUN,
ATEN'S DISK with outstretched arms and
hands as rays of light

DAWN

1
Dawn comes, sacred softening blue,
without a word, only the drone
of fan and 'fridge, the call
of a distant bird, the round balls
of the sky shift, and draft, and slide,
the solar thrust moves
mountains, sparks waves, propels songs.

Then gray clouds roll in,
rolls and a crack of thunder,
a jag of lightning defines the sky,
the first sprinkly drops of rain,
timpani of thunder, the downpouring

of rain washing Kristos feet,
Mary's endless wet fingers bathing,
bathing the feet of the world asking for peace,
asking for forgiveness, giving—
standing up to a clean slate of day!

Dawn comes, sacred dawn,
comes a benevolent cleansing rain
feeding the souls of the people
to sojourn, soul journey
with motion and love, stillness and prayer,
rapt in a robe of flesh.
The sun's heart having broken the black of night
now beams the eternal flame,
the steed unhitching their leather leads,
both stud and mare heralding
the galloping pace,
the womb of time, one more time
putting forth the plenitude,
the patter of feet upon well-trodden
wooden floors, mystic carpets,

the roll of rubber tires on ever-reaching
asphalt roadways to destinations
dreamed, now realities of touch and smell
and sight and sound and taste
of rainwater massaging the gums,
and swigged within the smacking of soft lips
soothing the hard and once yellowed teeth!

Yes, dawn comes, sacred softening rosy,
the dawning of dreams and of the flesh,
the dawning of mind and of the spirit,
of a new day,
of barnyards and bordellos,
break-fasts and mass starvation,
silk roads and naked children,
the neatly sheltered and the homeless.

Dawn comes, sacred radiant outreach,
through darkness, through darkened clouds, and spattered
rain...
radiant outreach of extending arms

from behind brightening horizon
to visible light hands reaching out
ever-widening fingers reaching out
fingertips touching—touching
anew!

2
With hands as warm as cool-morning coffee,
with fingers holding cigarette, to smoke, to sky.....
with Bird-song twittering the One bright Sun
      Once more Up

and, over the rim of land-ocean to sky,
                  night-dream to day

With memory and smell of dream-world
still tangled in daybreak hair
like the rustled worn beauty with the Lover,
an unkempt earthiness

      Once more Up

and, over the rim of a cup, a wall, a place
you were trying to hide behind

               over the rim

                   irrepressible

                      love of day!

3
Reaches out—
shines arms and hands and fingers forth,
the literal beams that awaken us,
and illuminate the fevered brow,
and soften human-kind's harshness,
Illuminating the ignorant spurts,
Illuminating the thankful groans,
reaching out from the dream,
riding the beams of Radiant Illumination,
the seasonal Illuminations
and veritable tracts of light,

the corridors of time,
protecting light bodies
giving strength, yet none too much...

the mushroom hats, and overreach of arbored leaves,
the husks and skins, the seeds and nutshells,
the rinds and pods,
shrubs, porches, and canopies
that protect all growing bounties,
protect us from Your scorching prowess,
protect us from your seasonal heatings and coolings,
as we orbit your center
with our own dance of colored cloudscapes and tinted skies,
our own dance of distance and approach,
give and take, dark and light.

The opening and closing of heliotropic flowers,
shadow and light and all shades of color,
Thou brighten deep green leaves with your unbiased shine,
all sway and dance to Your gradations,
the fabled shafts of light,
sparkling eyes, to goldfish glittering,
moistness of iris, to near-blinding waters,
rainbowed eyelash, to six-foot sunflowers,

from halo to harvest,
corona to cornfield,
aureole to orioles,
aura to oracle,
to aurora borealis to the north,
to aurora, Eos, goddess of the dawn, to the east,
to aurora australis to the south,
                    all day
until the last benevolent ray of light
from the last delicate touch
of the recoiling fingertip
from the outreaching hands
from the outreaching arms
from the Disk
of Aten!

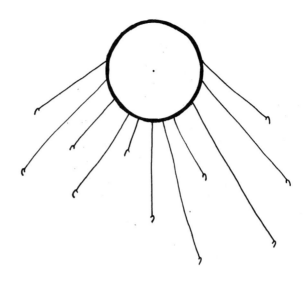

MID-MORNING

Once
we were eyes to eye
You

just above the endless circular horizon
the sparrows bolting playfully
from their once dark abodes,
the raucous crows
just above the blazing sunrise,
the doves' white bellies
gulls' white wing-spans
sharply reflecting Your early rays,
the bright cardinal amidst bushes
watching his olive-feathered, orange-beak lover
safely eat her seeds,
the golden goldfinches
rising chirps
just above the treetops

Thou
push ever-upwards
spreading and sending us

on our ways,
some forgetting Your beneficent rays,
instead immersing themselves with busied days,
yet some ever-mindful of Your presence

209

Mid-morning Sun
how far Your arms reach now
stretched across pale-blue skies
to green fields bathed
with cornstalk shadow and light
on farmer's bent back,
on street peddler's lined hand extended

Thou reach your arms and hands *far* now
almost touching
every thing
every dank corner
every sense
warming pores,
not quite your brightest moment
there is more
there is climax to reach,
directly overhead

where even Your full-bodied embrace
becomes oblivious
to all distinctions

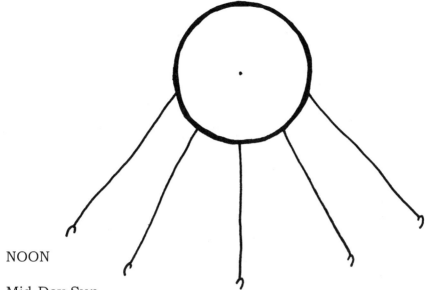

NOON

Mid-Day Sun
overhead
equal Radiant
Illumination,

center-point of sky,
center-point of dome of heavens,

cycle of clock,
of the round clock's two hands holding hands as one,
one upward pointing ray,

in prayer to the heavens,
human hands over heart in prayer

then raised above head,
arms-wide and curved
with sun-salutation, opening to

that One
spurring moment

and time moves on
with prayer ever-shining,
all day of Radiant Illumination
of long awaited light!

AFTERNOON

Your primal urge dispersed,
riding the light
of this very moment,
fed with shiny particles of radiant illumination

Once coursing into grains of pyramidal sand,
that even now, urge us onward
through dusty afternoons and labored roads,
the song still singing
across centuries of moments of revelation
to our open hearts,
soothing hubbub and softening brow,
guiding traffic and calmly, urgent voices...
    How is that so?
    How so, you have journeyed this far?

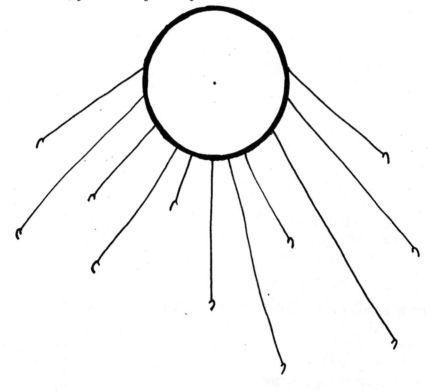

SUNDOWN

The day-galloping steed....
slowing to canter, to trot, to walk--
the moist, wide eyes illuminating,

and with a neigh and a nod
drawn to the corral,
humbly to the place

where hooves meet softened bed of straw-floor,
to buckets of water,
a hand of sugar,
the whinnied perfection.

To the lively pub
lifting an elbow
as the golden ball sinks, sinks
with measured precision

as if it would always be there
to guide us, the golden halo
holds itself almost motionless

with one last spread of wings,
of outreached arms
as if to say, 'I have given you everything I could.'

Your light hangs on
seemingly endlessly

suddenly embraces itself
then slides behind the rimmed horizon
and is gone

leaving only an incandescent trail
to find our homes,
with day's warmth tingling
on our pulsing skins,

the hoof beats reverberating
in the chambers of ears...

You are elsewhere now
gone, gone from direct sight,

leaving Your daily legacy
on Moon,
on sun-blanched hair,
on freckled face...

The distant stars
pale before Your shrine!
Until the last benevolent ray of radiant light
from the last delicate touch
of the recoiling fingertip
from the outreaching hands
from the outreaching arms
      from the Disk   of Aten!

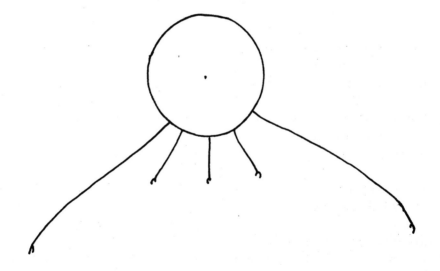

NIGHT-TIME

Long gone from sight
reflecting on the day's journey:

remedying what was out of reach
or unjustly broached upon a fellow human being,
learning from mistakes,

then, noting what was blessed this day—
the memory of children playing among such serious adults,
the flock of doves that lifted suddenly
in wavy unison from the upper branches of a tree,
the glint of youth still sparkling from the old man's eyes,
the way the road turned 'just so'
so you could see the moon perched on the darkening horizon,
the ring of telephone just after
the thought of the caller floated through your humble brain,
the warm stew stirred lovingly
on the hot stove whose tamed fire coaxed you to cook,
whose brightening flame puts food to your belly,
whose golden glow reminds you of the One bright Sun,
    Once more Up
        and over the landscape,
    Once more Down
        behind the rim of evening
while never really moving all the while.

We give thanks to You for all seasons!

.....as butterfly alights on bedpost,
as in our snugly tucked cocoon of blankets
we wonder what the day will bring,
what butterfly of light will sing across another dawn,
what place, what friend, what stranger, what moment
yearns for our warm touch
and bright spark of eye,
what burning desire, what gentle flame
seeks to mingle
with the light we have harvested within,
a light we have tilled and planted,
cultivated and sprouted forth
under Your ever-watchful days.

FOR THE 4 RACES UNITED

The quiet endurance of the black-soil earth
from Egypt's ancient riverbed,
and Homo Sapien's reported birth
from Africa's tribal watershed.

The Africans dis-placed onto foreign soil
enslaved then freed after many tears;
the American Indians dis-placed on their home soil,
quarantined, yet only freed by their own seers.

Were they not first,
the swarthy ones?
Were they not first, with East India,
the black-skin, black-brown, and brown-red skin
daughters and sons?

Now, perhaps the African-Americans
can show us all how to overcome the new slavery, so subtle,
of minimum wage and unaffordable housing—
it's time to 'pop' that karma-bubble.

The White-man's hinge hangs
on a rusted dinosaur door:
enslaved the Blacks, dis-placed the Reds, pangs...
and on the Golds in Japan, Vietnam and Korea waged war.

Throughout history
military and religious crusaders,
masquerading (it's no mystery)
as worldly saviors.

May some white blacksmith
forge a rust-proof hinge
in a red hot fire 'til there sparkles gold—
and end this rabid supremacy binge!

No turning back. What good regret?
Not just on White-man to pin the blame.
Clear Prism refracting Rainbow of Colors,
our Origin is all the same.

What destiny returns through prism?
What destiny upon this Earth?
To walk the Path of Worldly Lover
no price to put upon true self-worth!

SINGING AN EPIC OF PEACE

We are the reflections
Of Radiant Illumination
A True state of Being.

We brighten our reflections
With spiritual states and prayer,
Meditative-ness while active,

Clear state of mind,
With highest thoughts arising

in our feet and legs, and buttocks, our loins, our hips and guts,
and organs, our hearts, our chest and shoulders and arms, and
throats, our faces, minds and eyes and third-eyes,
and tops of heads.....

Guiding our actions and responses.

Savoring the physical
Pleasures of all the senses
And the sharing of these senses

With other Radiant Beings,
Heightens our experiences
Of Oneness

Giving Radiance
To All Light-Beings—
We live this Oneness.....

Singing an Epic of Peace
Of the Deity that speaks
From unending hidden crevices
And wide-open gathering places,
And from the central pillar
That spirals through us each
Without cease
With devoted ease.

If there is failure, keep on—
If success, keep on.

If there is failure, sing another song—
If success, sing along

Singing an Epic of Peace

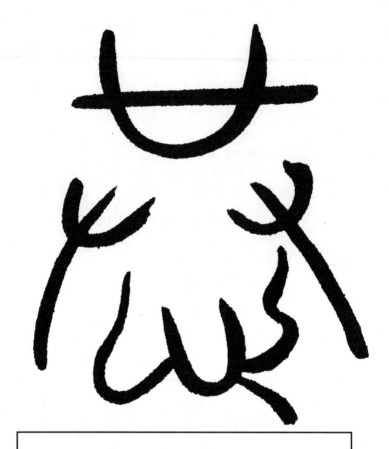

"RESPECTFUL"

"Twenty" ('ten'(+) plus 'ten') **+ plus + = ⊎**
"Pairs of Hands"
    working together
        and
showing Respect to others
            "Heart"

AFTER-WORDS:
THE END AND THE BEGINNING

There is a time when,
There is a place where,
There is no need for words.....

****

ADDENDUM

*Now that this 'literary' journey is complete, and you have become a 'hero' of sorts, here are a few ideas (along with those in the **Introductory Notes**) that you may find appliable to various parts of your life.*

Also listed below are some of the 'mechanics' of poetry that help to carry this song along.

AFTER-NOTES

EDUCATIONAL PROSPECTS
Many current Art forms and educational study courses would do well to encourage more blending with various other art forms. This happens naturally with any collaborative event, (even some dictionaries have photos, pictures and charts.) But a further encouragement of these types of blending would, in my humble opinion, make for more enjoyable forms of expression, as well as make for easier and more enjoyable educational systems, and easier for students to learn and process information, as well as cultivate enjoyable and conscious experiences. While learning the anatomy of a turtle, for example, one's interest might be piqued and knowledge broadened by also studying the mythology, cultural meanings, and artistic representations of Turtles, and vice versa.

Looking to the Muses would certainly provide some valuable insights and fresh approaches along these lines (or curves) both educationally and for the simple pleasures of learning.

FURTHER NOTES ON THE MUSES
One method of approaching the Muses would be to talk with, pray to, ask guidance from-- the specific Muse that suits your particular purpose. If you are writing about nature, there is Thaleia. If you want to bring more history into your work, there is Kleio. If you are a dancer or want your art or writings 'to dance', or want to 'dance' through a series of difficult business meetings, there is Terpsikhore....and so forth.

There are some classical and modern artworks that portray the various Muses; having pictures of them is one way to further connect. And as sisters are wont to chat it up amongst themselves, remember that the Muses 'mingle', though each has its specific traits and fields of expertise.

THE VERSE FORMS OF THIS POEM
The main verse forms used are:
Couplet (2-liners).

American (English-language) variations on **Haiku**; **Haikai-no-Renga**, or "linked verse", and **Tanka** (5-liners).

Ballad (quatrains with 2nd and 4th line rhyme).

Free Verse with various **Freeform Rhymed and Unrhymed** (with emphasis on modern 'beat or 'beatific' rhythm—which has become a standard of modern poetry forms.)

CULTURAL ASSOCIATIONS WITH THE FORMS

Couplet: classical English - Alexander Pope, the most well known.

Japanese **Haiku** and Haikai No Renga (linked verse 5-7-5/7-7/5-7-5/7-7 etc. loosely, and Tanka. The numbers represent Japanese 'sound-symbols' that have been used as a format for 'English' syllables, though most modern Haiku societies and poets agree on various shorter syllabic-forms, (3-5-3 for example,) as better equating with the 'sounds' of Japanese. Whatever the specific form, these styles at their highest reflect the philosophies of Zen Buddhism, Buddhism, and Taoism.

Originally haiku were called "haikai no renga" and were 'linked-verses' often composed by several writers, or as communications between friends. Individual haiku are reflective of humor, 'AHA! moments', subtle or meditative awareness - 'AH-ness', and riddle or Koan-like contemplations. As to the length of haiku they are said to be 'a breath's worth'-- "....the number of syllables that can be uttered in a breath makes the natural length."[123]

Yet, perhaps the truest haiku-sounds can be gleaned from the little twitters and calls of birds.

Ballad: Narrative poem or song. There are numerous forms of poetic ballads, especially from Italy. I have used quatrains where the 2nd and 4th lines rhyme, and adopted a loose ballad form, varying standard meters to help prevent excess repetitive sing-song refrain. Folk ballads were sung and passed down through generations. Most associate ballads with songs. The Old Provençal word-root of ballad is "balada" 'song sung while dancing'. Spanish "bailar" is 'to dance'. Two modern American Masters of song ballads and song storytelling are Pete Seeger and Bob Dylan.

Beat poetry: Made popular and defined by Jack Kerouac, along with Allen Ginsberg, Lawrence Ferlinghetti, and others, notably in the 1950s San Francisco area. 'Beat' poetry brought forth an expression of 'counter culture', offering more musically inspired rhythms, as compared with the more intellectual and classically-referenced poetry of academia. Beat-ific poetry, and its stream of consciousness, perhaps owes as much to Walt Whitman, Dylan Thomas, and even as far back as the original "Great Hymn to the Aten/Hymn to the Sun", or the original Oratory transmission of poetry.

Beat-ific is: of beauty, beatitude, blessing and bliss. Therefore, I regard the highest aim of this style as a chanting, hymn-like stream of consciousness aimed at an overall vision and experience of beauty. Much "beat" poetry deals with various everyday difficulties and the sometimes seamy side of things, and I feel that this is the poet's attempt to come to terms with certain conditions and ultimately help lift the mood to a higher level of transcendence, hence "beat-ific".
(my interpretation of what Jack Kerouac meant by calling it that.[124])

While 'beat' can also mean "weary, broke, homeless, exhausted, emptied out" (and hence the tendency for some poets to accentuate this level,) perhaps the true work of a 'beat poet' is somewhat like that of an alchemist— transmuting his own 'beaten-ness' into a 'a blessing, beatitude, bliss, and ultimately-- a Beatific Vision'.

The 'beat' poets' freeform style helped to revolutionize 'modern' poetry. The affects of the 'beat generation' can be seen and heard poetically nowadays with numerous performance poetry readings, and spoken-word artists. Beat-poetry accentuates a certain Street-Wisdom; a celebration of one's unique personal (as well as universal) Vision; and a breaking-free from societal and poetic norms. The 'beats' also touch upon the spiritual and monastic archetypes of Buddhism, wandering Zen monks, and the monastic or temple life as a means of being at peace with one's situation, and unattached to material gain and worldly affairs.

Free Verse: with various non-traditional rhymed and un-rhymed.

Rap/Hip-Hop: occasional extended rhyming-flow that seemingly blends the Beat-ific and more traditional rhyme rhythms and cadences, though creating a distinctly modern, urban rhythm—the voice of a culture, with uplift from urban demise and poverty. Though many current rap/hip-hop themes revolve around sexuality and materiality, some of the higher levels of awareness (as seen with most arts) use this form to 'speak' for equality, and to shed light on dark corners of any 'systems' of oppression. As an overall poetic/song movement, I consider rap/hip-hop a communal voice and rhythm, much like the inspirational songs sung by slave-workers to keep their spirits up while doing hard labor. Though the labor may not be slave labor anymore, some of the rap/hip-hop voices sing out AGAINST slave wages, oppression, bigotry, violence, etc. and sing FOR affirmations of a culture's rhythm, self-esteem, spirit, and liberation.

Jazz, The Blues, and other musical forms provide similar functions, and each has its own artistic merit. As some Jewish people sing while working on diamonds; as some Tibetan people sing while tamping/dancing on the dusty roof-work of a village home-- each culture and people have songs that are woven into the fabric of their lives.

Hymns: poetic songs of praise.

Other stylistic influences, with gratitude for the poetic expressions from—
the sounds of Gerard Manley Hopkins; the simplicity and playfulness of Dorothy Parker and Ogden Nash; the clarity of Rudyard Kipling; the energy and boldness of Walt Whitman, who is quoted as writing: the true job of the poet is to "cheer up slaves, and horrify despots" (to which I add— help *liberate* slaves...); Robert Burns' theme of poems against secular tyrannies, as well as FOR equality; the visceral and spiritual quality of Rumi; e.e. cummings for showing that anything is possible; Gary Snyder's simplicity, nobility, and love of Mother Earth; Tibetan Buddhist spiritual verses; and worldwide poetry and mythologies.

ENDNOTES

[1] Aluna Joy Yaxk'in, "Mayan Prophesy The Reawakening Of The Cosmic Human" &
Steve McFadden, "The Tale Of Our Pilgrimage To The South", 1995, The Wisdom Conservancy.<http://www.v-j-enterprises.com/mayanpr.html> (date site accessed: 25 Aug 2003)
Steven McFadden, "Solar Cermonies Set for 1995 Spring Equinox: March 21, 1995 marks completion of 520-year-old Mayan prophecy" *Odyssey,* March 1995. (not sure this newspaper from Maine/New Hampshire is still being published).

[2] "New York State Racing and Wagering Board: Indian Gaming" <http://www.racing.state.ny.us/Indian/FAQ.html> (4 July 2003)
"Sovereignty: Historical and Cultural Origins" Official site of the Coeur d'Alene Tribe, Idaho, 2003. <http://www.cdatribe.org/sovereignty.html> (22 June 2003)
"Americn Indian Tribal Sovereignty Primer "(various links), American Indian Policy Center, St. Paul, MN, 2002. <http://www.airpi.org/pubs/index.html#sov> (5 July 2003)
"Native Tribes of the United States and Canada" listing Federally recognized and State recognized, site maintained by JS Dill. <http://www.dickshovel.com/trbindex.html> (29 July 2003)

[3] < http://www.racing.state.ny.us/Indian/FAQ.html>

[4] "Native American Prophecies Fulfilled: "North American Indian Prophecies" " - - excerpts from a talk given by Lee Brown (Baha'i- Cherokee) at the 1986 Baha'i Continental Indigenous Council, Fairbanks, Alaska. <http://www.bci.org/prophecy-fulfilled/nativeam.htm> (2 Oct. 2002)

[5] U.S. Census Bureau, International Database and The World Factbook, 2001.

[6] Walt Whitman poem

[7] from "Kalevala" Runo I (Opening verses or Proem - the Finnish national epic, collected and trans. Elias Lonnrot, 1835; English trans. W.F. Kirby 1907) <www.abo.fi/instut/iamsr/waeno/kalevala.html> (19 June 2003)

[8] "The Strange Origin of Corn: an Abenaki Legend", Brown. "Journal of American Folklore" on website <http://www.earthbow.com/native/abenaki/strangecorn.htm> (29 June 2003)

[9] Amaruca articles:
"The Great God Pan is Not Dead". <http://www.crosscircle.com/Humanity'sVisionOfGod.htm> (3 June 2003)
"Luis Valdez Discusses Cultural Inclusiveness and Indian Roots in the United States" <http://www.radiobilingue.org/luisvaldez.htm> (3 June 2003)
"North American Snake Worship" <http://www.stargods.org/NorthAmericanSnake.htm> (3 June 2003)

[10] Judith Nies, *Native American History* (NY: Ballantine Books, 1996), pp.42-44.

[11] Howard Zinn, *A People's History of the United States* (NY: Perennial Classics, HarperCollins Publishers, 1980, 2001), pp.96-102.

[12] "The Moral Washington: Construction of a Legend (1800-1920s)" <http://xroads.virginia.edu/~CAP/gw/gwmoral.html> (29 July 2003)

[13] Roy Blount Jr. host, Roger Weisberg prod. and dir., Stephen Segaller exec. prod. Thirteen/WNET NY documentary *The Main Stream* premiered 17 Dec. 2002 on PBS.

14 "A Resource for the Upper Mississippi River"
<http://www.oldmanriver.com> (7 Nov. 2002)
"The Mississipppi by any other name"
<http://www.oldmanriver.com/Pages/name.htm> (7 Nov. 2003)

15 "Michigan"
<www.shabbir.com/nonmatchbox/states/michigan.html> (8 Nov. 2002)
"Named in 1805, apparently for Lake Michigan; itself named from an Indian
word, possibly Chippewa Michigama "great lake," or possibly from mishi-maikin-
nac "swimming turtle," descriptive of Mackinac Island. Early 18th Century maps
of North America vary, some labeling present-day Lake Huron as Lake Michigan
(and labeling the latter as Lake Illinois), but present naming practice is seen on
maps regularly after 1757."

16Michel Gros-Louis, linguist, "Huron-Wendat Language", 1999.
<http://www.agondachia.com/langue.html> (18 Jan. 2003)

17 "The Huron Indians", paragraph "Names" and "Huron Location",
<www.members.tripod.com/paullife/huronindians.html> (18 Jan. 2003)

18 Bruce Grant, Concise Encyclopedia of the American Indian - revised edition
(NY: Wings Books 1958, 1960, E.P. Dutton & Co., Inc.), p. 203.

19 The Missouri(a) call themselves "Nau'tatci"
<http://hotcakencyclopedia.com/ho.GlossaryIndianNations.html>
(website note: Most of the information found here was taken from Carl
Waldman, Encyclopedia of Native American Tribes, revised edition (New
York: Checkmark Books, 1999.)) (24 June 2003)

20 Ken Burns, dir. and prod., Dayton Duncan, prod. and co-writer, Geoff
Ward, co-writer, PBS TV Documentary Mark Twain (first aired 14/15 Jan. 2002)

21 Addison Erwin Sheldon "History and Stories of Nebraska" - Part 2 Chapter 3,
'Nebraska Indians As The White Men Found Them', Oldtime Nebraska.
<http://www.ku.edu/~kansite/hvn/books/nbstory/nbstory3.html>
(26 April 2002)

22David Hackett (Yuchi historian) "Who were the mysterious Yuchi Indians of
Tennessee and the Southeast? : The Bat Creek Stone"
<http://www.drwebman.com/euchee/yuchi/>(10 Nov. 2002)
Bill Baker "Tennessee: The Origin of Our State's Name".
<http://www3.tellico.net/~tellicotimes/Tenn.html> (10 Nov. 2002)
"Yuchi" (Georgia) Extract from The Indian Tribes of North America
by John R. Swanton Bureau of American Ethnology Bulletin 145—1953
[726 pages—Smithsonian Institution](pp. 104-120) -website The Northern
Plains Archive Project 12/29/99.
<http://hiddenhistory.com/PAGE3/SWSTS/georgia1.htm>(22 Feb. 2003)

23 "Mexican Holidays: Cinco de Mayo"
<www.mexonline.com/cinco.htm> (23 Feb. 2002)
"Cinco de Mayo" <http://latino.sscnet.ucla.edu/demo/cinco.html>
(9 March 2002)

24 Star Trek Vulcan blessing.

25 "Christopher Gist's Journals with Historical, Geographical and Ethnological
Notes and Biographies of His Contemporaries by William M. Darlington
[1815-1889] Pittsburgh, J.R. Weldin& Co. 1893 [Part4.]"
US GenWeb Archives Pennsylvania.
<http://www.rootsweb.com/~usgenweb/pa/1pa/1picts/gist/gj4b.html>
(29 June 2003)

Patsy Woodring,"Indian Old Fields, Home of the Shawnee" and her bibliography, 2001. <http://www.kentuckyexplorer.com/nonmembers/01-04020.html> (14 Feb. 2002)

26 James Duvall, M.A. (and bibliography), "A Note on a Mistaken Date for the Discovery of Big Bone Lick" (website reference: "Note: Another historian besides Jillson who got the date correct was Archibald Henderson, Ph.D., The Conquest of the Old Southwest: The Romantic Story of the Early Pioneers into Virginia, The Carolinas, Tennessee, and Kentucky 1740-1790, (1920; rpt. Spartanburg, S.C., Reprint Co., 1974), chapt. 8:" <http://www.geocities.com/boonehistory/1729-note.html> (14 Feb. 2003)
Nancy Bray, submitted by. "Historical Winchester and Vicinity", website 2000-2003 <www.rootsweb.com/~kyclark/winchester.html> (14 Feb. 2003)

27 Col. John Johnston, Indian Agent, originally publ. in 1858 "Vocabularies of the SHAWANOESE AND WYANDOTT LANGUAGES, ETC." <http://www.sfo.com/~denglish/wynaks/lang1.html> (22 Feb. 2003)

28 "The Commonwealth of Kentucky" Kentucky Atlas and Gazetteer. <www.uky.edu/KentuckyAtlas/kentucky.html> (10 Nov. 2002)

29 Nies, pp. 388-89.

30 Lee Sultzman "Niantic History", revised 7.15.1997 <www.dickshovel.com/nian.html> (1 March 2003)

31 "About Mohegan Sun > About the Tribe > sacred turtle" <http://www.mohegansun.com/about/the_tribe.jsp> (27 Jan. 2003) "13 Moons in the Mohegan Year" <http://www.mohegan.nsn.us/tribe/c200content.html> (27 Jan. 2003)

32 Paula Giese, "Treaties with Minnesota Indians", 1997. <www.kstrom.net/isk/maps/mn/treaties.html> (18 Nov. 2002)

33 "What's in a Name", River Warren Research Committee, from other historical references. <http://www.riverwarren.com/page.asp?page=whatsinname>(15Feb.'03)

34 "The Upper Dells", Glacier Valley Wilderness Tours. <http://www.glaciervalley.com/wisconsi.htm> (25 July 2003)
"History of Wisconsin Dells : A Native American Legend", Downtown Wisconsin Dells. 1995-2002. <http://downtown-dells.com/history.htm> (16 Feb. 2003) "History and Origin of Wisconsin Dells, Wisconsin!" (9-16-2002/1995-2003 Ad-Lit Inc.) <http://www.dells.com/dellshistory/> (16 Feb. 2003)

35 Dennis McCann of the Milwaukee Journal Sentinel Staff, "As nation hungered for wood, Wisconsin's pine seemed endless". <www.jsonline.com/news/state/wis150/stories/0621sesqui.stm> (17 Feb. 2003)

36 Lee Sultzman, "Winnebago History" 9-30-2000. <www.dickshovel.com/win.html> (29 July 2003)
"The Ho-Chunk Nation: A Brief History" <www.ho-chunknation.com/heritage/culture_history_page.htm>(28 July 2003)

37 Murton L. McCluskey, Ed. D. Great Falls, MT distributed by Nancy Keenan, Superintendent, Office of Public Instruction PO Box 202501, Helena, MT 59620-2501 (revised 1997) <http://216.239.39.100/search?q=cache:RUxR0_1ZDkQJ:www.opi.state.mt.us/PDF/IndianEd/IndianEdCurricGuide.pdf+ogwa+peon&hl=en&ie=UTF-8> (29 July 2003) ("ogwa peon")
Murton L. McCluskey, Ed. D. Great Falls, MT distributed by Nancy Keenan,

Superintendent, Office of Public Instruction PO Box 202501, Helena, MT 59620-2501 (revised 1997) p.15. <http://www.opi.state.mt.us/PDF/IndianEd/IndianEdCurricGuide.pdf> (29 July 2003)

38 "Meaning of a Place Name: Oregon" <http://www.sacklunch.net/placenames/O/Oregon.html> (29 June 2003)

39 "Oregon Origin", The AFU and Urban Legend Archive Language Etymology (electronic bulletin board - Re: What does "Oregon" mean? (22 Nov 1995) <http://www.urbanlegends.com/language/etymology/oregon_origin.html> (29 June 2003)

"Oregon Facts: Interesting Names and Places in Oregon - The Oregon Name Controversy"<http://www.webtrail.com/applegate/oregon.html> (29 June 2003)

40 David Lewis, member of the Confederated Tribes of Grand Ronde, and Scott Byram, works with Coquille Tribe and other Indian communities, "Indian Trade Route Lead to Overlooked Origin of 'Oregon' ". Univ. of Oregon Campus News with link to above. <http://www.uoregon.edu/newscenter/oregon.html> (29 June 2003)

41 <http://www.sacklunch.net/placenames/O/Oregon.html>

42 Marisa Agha, "FOUNDATIONS: Indian group provides grant Klamath Tribes to receive $115,000" Pioneer Press, posted 3-29-03. (website: Indian Land Tenure Foundation,>"Newspaper Articles", 2002-2003.) <http://www.indianlandtenure.org/news/news.html> (8 Sept. 2003)

43 Lee Sultzman, "Comanche History". <http://www.tolatsga.org/ComancheOne.html> (29 July 2003)

44 "States with Indian Names" SouthCoast Repertory Playgoer's Guide. <http://www.scr.org/season/0203season/studyguides/indiansummer/classroom.html> (13 June 2003) <http://www.scr.org> (29 July 2003)

"Facts - States with Indian Names" Department of Cultural Affairs: Nevada Kids Page. <http://dmla.clan.lib.nv.us/docs/kids/in-names.htm> (18 June 2003)

Bruce Grant, p.157. (Shoshoni word.)

45 Dennis Kucinich (D.-Ohio) proposal H.R. 1673 for a U.S. Peace Dept. Introdcued 4-8-03, Campaign for U.N. Reform <http://www.cunr.org/priorities/108th/H.R.%201673%20%20Dept%20of%20Peace.htm> (June 2003)

46 Official site of the Coeur d'Alene Tribe <http://www.cdatribe.org/>

47 "The Meaning of Arizona", Arizona State Library, Archives and Public Records, (with sources listed) 2/02. <http://www.lib.az.us/links/Azmeaning.htm> (28 July 2003)

48 Jeffrey Scott, "Pima Indians" 7/03 <http://jeff.scott.tripod.com/pima.html> (11 Oct.2002)

"Arizona Government and General History: Arizona's Name" source: Granger, Byrd Howell Arizona's Names: X Marks the Place Falconer Pub. Co. 1983, Tucson, AZ. distributed by Treasure Chest Publications. (from website: <http://jeff.scott.tripod.com/azhistory.html> (28 July 2003)

49 "The Meaning of "Ali-Shonak" Amigos de Arizonac <http://www.azamigos.com/Meaningx.html> (28 July 2003)

"Arizona Government and General History: Arizona's Name" <http://jeff.scott.tripod.com/azhistory.html>

"You are right!" Southern Arizona <http://www.geocities.com/southernarizona3/Youareright.htm>(28July 2003)

Donald T. Garate fr. "State Names" 1998-2002. More information about this
theory can be found in the article, "Who Named Arizona? The Basque
Connection" in the Journal of Arizona History, July 1999 Edition by Donald
T. Garate,
<http://www.namely-yours.com/namesstates.php#ARIZONA%20-%20(AZ)>
<http://www.namely-yours.com/namesstates.php> (28 July 2003)1998-
2002, (host site) <www.mysunnycorner.com>

50 Donald T. Garate (from " State Names - Arizona") & Buber.net "Basque Word
List" maintained by Blas Uberuaga
<http://www.buber.net/Basque/Euskara/hitz.html> (15 Feb. 2003)
Morris Dictionary
(Azken eguneratzea: 2001-10-26
Kultura Saila
Hizkuntza Politikarako Sailburuordetza)
<http://www1.euskadi.net/morris/resultado.asp> (15 Feb. 2003)

51 Penfield Gallery of Indian Arts, Albuquerque, NM, 2002.
<www.penfieldgallery.com/sand.html> (28 July 2003)

52 "Long Walk", go to site Black Mesa Indigenous Support, then "Background"
then "Long Walk.<http://www.blackmesais.org> (site note: This article was
copied from http://www.navajo.org/lwalk.html, their server is often down
so it is reprinted here as it appears on their site. This page is a product of
The Agency Network Program under the Office of the Speaker.updated 1999.)
<www.blackmesais.org/longwalk> (17 Nov. 2002)

53 "Kaw Nation of Oklahoma" (ak'a).
<http://www.trailsoftears.net/tribalinfo/content-kaw.htm> (2 July 2003)

54 Kaw Nation site sections "History" "Culture" "Kaw History by William E.
Unrau". <http://www.kawnation.com> (3 March 2002)

55 Alma M. Herman, trans fr. German to English "Russian Germans on the
Canadian Prairie" North Dakota State University Libraries, Viktor Peters
6-8-1990 <http://www.lib.us.ndsu.nodak.edu/grhc/history_culture/
history/peters2.html> (25 June 2003)
Norman E. Saul "The Migration of the Russian-Germans to Kansas" Kansas
Collection: Kansas Historical Quarterlies, Spring, 1974 (Vol.40, No. 1), from
Kansas State Historical Society.
<http://www.kancoll.org/khq/1974/74_1_saul.htm> (25 June 2003)

56 Leonard Peltier, U.S. prisoner #89637-132, ed. by Harvey Arden,
Prison Writings: My Life Is My Sun Dance (NY: St. Martin's Griffin, 1999)
(Peltier was born on Turtle Mountain Reservation, North Dakota.)

57 "A People..." Eagle's Wings Ministry.
<http://www.eagles-wingsmin.com/senamc1.htm> (26 July 2003)
"First Nations Peoples" 1996-2003 <http:www.snowhawk.com/fn.html>
(2 March 2003)

58 Ann Maloney, "Migration of the Indian Tribes" OK Gen Web, The US Gen
Web Project, Bartlesville, OK, 1998.
<www.rootsweb.com/~oknowata/Migra.htm> (31 Oct. 2001)

59 Muriel H. Wright, "Chronicles of Oklahoma,Volume 14, No. 2, June, 1936,
CONTRIBUTIONS OF THE INDIAN PEOPLE TO OKLAHOMA, p156"
Oklahoma Historical Society's and OSU Library Electronic Publishing Center's
Chronicles of Oklahoma, Oklahoma State University Edmon Low Library
<http://digital.library.okstate.edu/Chronicles/v014/v014p156.html>

or seacrh website (28 July 2003)

[60] "Oklahoma History" Oklahoma City Convention & Visitors Bureau,
<www.okccvb.org/history/ok_history.htm> (2 March 2003)

[61] Nies, p. 226.

[62] Maloney, "The Native Tribes" US Gen Web Project, 1998.
<http://www.rootsweb.com/~oknowata/NatTri.htm> (31 Oct. 2001)

[63] Standing Bear Online, "The Six Tribes: The Tonkawa Nation".
<www.north-ok.edu/sb/six_tribes/6f_tonkawa_nation_1_5.htm>(26 April 2002)

[64] Nies, pp. 242-5 & 310.

[65] Paula Giese, "Treaties with Minnesota Indians" 1997
<http://www.kstrom.net/isk/maps/mn/treaties.html> (18 Nov. 2002)

[66] Nies pp. 258-60.

[67] Andrew Metz, Staff Correspondent "A Struggle for History: A people who
survived now seek to thrive in the 21st century" *Newsday* online, 6-23-03
<http://www.newsday.com/news/nationworld/ny-usind0626,0,2041955.story>
(26 June 2003)

[68] "North Dakota Prairie: Our Natural Heritage", Northern Prairie Wildlife
Research Center from: North Dakota Parks and Recreation Department.
No Date. "North Dakota prairie: our natural heritage" North Dakota Parks
and Recreation Department, U.S. Department of the Interior, U.S. Fish and
Wildlife Service. Jamestown, ND: Northern Prairie Wildlife Research Center
Home Page. (Version 05MAY99),
<http://www.npwrc.usgs.gov/resource/1999/heritage/heritage.htm>
(1 March 2003)

[69] Mandan, Hidatsa, and Arikara Tribes <www.mhanation.com>
(1 March 2003) (note: Sioux, a name from other tribes, meaning "adders", as
does Iroquois (not their true names.)

[70] "Glossary of Indian Nations" (site note: Most of the information found here
was taken from Carl Waldman, Encyclopedia of Native American Tribes,
revised edition (New York: Checkmark Books, 1999).
<http://hotcakencyclopedia.com/ho.GlossaryIndianNations.html>
(20 Oct. 2002)

[71] Baxoje, The Ioway Nation - Ioway Cultural Institute :
The Ioway Virtual Library, *Tanji na Che*: Recovering the Landscape of the
Ioway, (1999 "*Tanji na Che*: Recovering the Landscape of the Ioway." In
Recovering The Prairie. Edited by Robert F. Sayre. University of Wisconsin
Press, 1999 by Lance M. Foster and the University of Wisconsin Press.) (and
reference to Mott Wedel, Mildred 1978 "A Synonym of Names for the Ioway
Indians" *Journal of the Iowa Archeological Society* 25:48-77. site updated
11-23-02.<http://ioway.nativeweb.org/iowaylibrary/tanji.htm>(25 July 2003)
"A Closing Circle: Musings on the Ioway Indians in Iowa." In *The Worlds
Between Two Rivers: Perspectives on American Indians* in Iowa. Pp. 142-150.
Edited by Gretchen M. Bataille, David Mayer Gradwohl, and Charles L. P.
Silet., 2000, Lance M. Foster and the University of Iowa Press. 11-23-02.
<http://ioway.nativeweb.org/iowaylibrary/circle.htm> (25 July 2003)
"The Ioway and the Landscape of Southeast Iowa" section "Landscape,
archaeology, and history" Ioway Cultural Institute : The Ioway Virtual
Library, The Ioway and the Landscape of Southeast Iowa.
Original publication information: Foster, Lance M. 1996. "The Ioway and the
Landscape of Southeast Iowa." Journal of the Iowa Archeological Society

43:1-5. Lance M. Foster 1996, site updated 11/23/2002.
<http://ioway.nativeweb.org/iowaylibrary/seiowa.htm>
site host: http://ioway.nativeweb.org (25 July 2003)

[72] Evan T. Pritchard *Native New Yorkers (San Francisco/Tulsa: Counicl Oak Books)*, 2002. p. 32.

[73] "Indiana: Fast Facts and Trivia - #16 " 50states.com Thanks to: Jack Daniels, Mandy Paige, Beth Markley, Pike Street Industries, Inc. 2003. < http://www.50states.com/facts/indiana.htm> (29 July 2003) or websearch "Indiana Fast Facts"

[74] "Indiana Territory -- Beginnings: The Origin of "Indiana" " 2000, 2002. Centennial History and Handbook of Indiana George S. Cottman, and A Survey of the State by Counties, Max R. Hyman.
7-26-03. <http://www.countyhistory.com/history/054.htm> (26 July 2003)

[75] Evan T. Pritchard, *No Word For Time: The Way of the Algonquin People* (San Francisco/Tulsa: Council Oak Books, 1997, (Appendix 2001)). Same info - "The Major Algonquin Nations Throughout North America and What They Call Themselves" <http://www/wilkesweb.net/cac-nations.htm> (6 July 2003)

[76] Lee Sultzman "Narragansett History" (revised 7-15-'97) see "Names" <http://www.dickshovel.com/Narra.html> (17 Feb. 2002)

[77] "ALABAMA-COUSHATTA INDIANS." The Handbook of Texas Online.
<http://www.tsha.utexas.edu/handbook/online/articles/view/AA/bma19.html> [Accessed Fri Jul 25 17:36:23 US/Central 2003]. or
<www.tsha.utexas.edu> and search "Coushatta Indians", then article#2.

[78] "Alabama" Source: Benjamin F. and Barbara S. Shearer *State Names, Seals, Flags and Symbols* (Westport, CT: Greenwood Press, 1994).
<http://www.netstate.com/states/intro/al_intro.htm> (29 July 2003)
"The Alabama State Name" ADAH (Alabama Department of Archives and History), updated 6-26-2001.
<http://www.archives.state.al.us/statenam.html> (22 July 2003)
"States with Indian Names" The People: Native American Legacy
<http://dmla.clan.lib.nv.us/docs/nsla/srp/people/chap4f.htm>(25 Oct.2002)

[79] R.E. Moore and Texarch Associates & "The Handbook of Texas Online" "The Alabama-Coushatta Indians" 1996-2001.
<http://www.texasindians.com/albam.htm> (25 Nov 2001)

[80] William A. Updike "Here We May Rest", National Parks Conservation Association
<http://www.npca.org/magazine/2001_issues/March_April/
Historic_Highlightsasp> (5 July 2003)
"The Alabama State Name"
<http://www.archives.state.al.us/statenam.html>
"Alabama And It's Hamlets"
<http://www2.pcom.net/cinjod/historian/Hamlets.html> (5 July 2003)

[81] source : Benjamin F. and Barbara S. Shearer State Names, Seals, Flags and Symbols Westport, CT: GreenWood Press, 1994).
1997-2003 <www.netstate.com> (29 July 2003)
"Origin of the Names of U.S. States" (source: State officials, the Smithsonian Institution, and the Topographic Division, U.S. Geological Survey.)
<http://www.klascement.net/aa/software/usaname.txt> (29 June 2003)

[82] Pritchard, pp. 30-31 & 349-50.

[83] Bruce Grant, p. 336. (Lenape village in Pennsylvania "M'cheuwomink". Perhaps also "Wishkonsing - "place of the beaver" or "muskrat hole".)

[84] Little Bighorn Battlefield National Monument, The Apsaalooke (Crow) Scouts, The National Park Service, May 2000.
<http://www.nps.gov/libi/apsaloo.html> (22 July 2003)
"Crow Tribal Council" Montana-Wyoming Tribal Leaders Council
<http://tlc.wtp.net/crow.htm> (29 July 2003)

[85] "Histories of the Utah Tribes" Utah Division of Indian Affairs 2002, (with sources listed).
<www.dced.state.ut.us/indian/History/history.htm> (9 Feb 2002)

[86] "Hawaiki" 7-26-03 <http://www.wikipedia.org/wiki/Hawaiki>
"Hawai'iki - The Ancient Land"
<http://www.spiritsouthseas.com/hawaiiki.htm> (7 July 2003)
"Re: Origin of the word "Hawaii"
<http://www.moolelo.com/talkstory/messages/632.html>(16 Feb. 2002)
(no longer there, perhaps www.moolelo.com or, www.hawaiination.org/moolelo.html)

[87] "Introduction to Hawaii" - The United States of America Netstate.com Source: Benjamin F. and Barbara S. Shearer *State Names, Seals, Flags and Symbols* (Westport, CT: Greenwood Press), 1994.
<http://www.netstate.com/states/intro/hi_intro.htm> (16 Feb 2002)

[88] United States Public Law 103-150, The "Apology Resolution" Passed by Congress and signed by President William J. Clinton, November 23, 1993,
<www.hawaii-nation.org/publawsum.html> (12 Aug. 2002)
"H A W A I ` I Independent & Sovereign" for more info.
<http://www.hawaii-nation.org> (27 July 2003)

[89] Zinn , pp. 310-12.

[90] James Loewen *Lies My Teacher Told Me* (NY: A Touchstone Book publ. by Simon & Schuster, 1995,1996), p.105.(he cites -- J. Leitch Wright, Jr., *The Only Land They Knew* (New York: Free Press, 1981), pp. 33, 130.)

[91] Official Site of the Sovereign Miccosukee Seminole Nation
<http://www.miccosukeeseminolenation.com/> (22 July 2003)

[92] California Tour and Travel, 2002.
<http://www.californiatourandtravel.com/archive.html> (27 June 2003)
caliph, calif, khalif, khalafa from Arabic "halafa"- 'to succeed', "halifa" - 'successor, be behind', as in various rulers or successors of Muhammed.

[93] all of these references mentioned in "Chronology of California History: 1757"
<http://www.walika.com/sr/cal-chron.htm> (5 March 2003)
also: "kali forno" = 'native land, or mountains, or high hills' from Baja Indians <http://www.californiatourandtravel.com/archive.html>

[94] Nies., pp. 197-98.

[95] "Gold, Greed & Genocide" <www.1849.org> for more information see documentary film or website (29 July 2003)

[96] "Welcome to Mexico: History" Fifth Global Conference for Health Promotion.
<http://www.who.int/hpr/conference/mexico/mexico.html>
<http://www.who.int/hpr/conference/index.html (home page)] (24 July 2003)
"Huitzilopochtli" from "The Aztecs - Section 2", Website of the Snaith Primary School, webmaster Derek Allen.
<http://home.freeuk.net/elloughton13/huiz.htm> (24 July 2003)

[97] Arturo Tena Colunga Ph. D., "Which is the meaning of the name of Mexico?" (with extensive references).
<www.public.iastate.edu/~rjsalvad/scmfaq/mexname.html> (17 Feb. 2003)

[98] Colunga. & "Amaryllis" The Columbia Encyclopedia, Sixth Edition, 2001.
<http://www.bartleby.com/65/am/amarylli.html> (18 Feb. 2003)

[99] Authors: Maria Jose Eguskiza Garai and Lourdes Gonza'lez-Bueno, Technical advisers of the Council of Education, Council of Education And Science. London. Publicaciones. Latin America. "Mexico, The Navel of the Moon" Latin Series America, No. 1, ("...house of dawn...")
<www.sgci.mec.es/uk/Pub/Mex/> (24 April 2003)

[100] This distinction hinges on the letters "B" and "F". Reportedly-Eburos from a Celtic name which was probably from Eboracum, from ancient Celtic word Eburos or Ebor "Yew tree", a sacred Celtic tree. Anglo-Saxon speech turned this into Eoforwic 'wild boar settlement' from Eofor "wild boar". Norse Jórvík, to English York. The New York state seal, along with the figures of an Indian and a Dutchman, has the words "Sigillum Civitatis Novi Eboraci" 'Sign of the city of New 'York'. Interpretations differ, yet (although perhaps idealistically,) I lean toward the "Yew-tree" interpretation, and, because of the "B".
"Johannes LeCanter of Wodemanse Manor, Beverly, East Riding, County York, England, In The Year 1297: "The Origin of York" ".
<http://www.members-tripod.com/~Drudge_J/Johannes.htm> (9 Nov. 2002)
David A. Simpson, North East England History Pages "City of York History", 1991-2001. <http://www.thenortheast.fsnet.co.uk/YorkCity.htm> (9 Nov. 2002)
"Archeology and Language" Source for this page: Kenneth Cameron, *English Place Names*. London: B.T. Batsford, 1963.
<http://english.ohiostate.edu/people/odlin.1/courses/774/arclg774.htm> (9 Nov. 2002)
"COLONIA EBORACENSIVM / EBVRACVM Roman Colony & Legionary Fortress, York, North Yorkshire: "Colonia Eboracensivm" "(modified 1-23-03) "Eburacum - The Place of Yews"--"York Eborakon c.150, Eboracum, Euruic 1086 (DB). An ancient Celtic name meaning 'estate of a man called Eburos' or (more probably) 'yew-tree estate'. Yorkshire (OE scir 'district') is first referred to in the 11th cent."
Entry from the Oxford Dictionary of English Place-Names by A.D. Mills. "The above statement by Mills is very difficult to reconcile with any of the relevant names for the Yew tree. The Latin name for yew is Taxus baccata, the modern English name stems from the Saxon iw, also the Germanic iwa and Scandinavian yr; also compare Welsh ywen. A possible clue lies in the modern German name for the tree, Eibe."
<http://www.roman-britain.org/places/eburacum.htm> (9 Nov. 2002)

[101] Pritchard, p. 74. "..in 1653, the Dutch built a palisaded wall to keep the Lenape out, site of today's Wall Street." & p. 129, Peter Stuyvesant.

[102] Pritchard, p. 20.

[103] (general history)
Lee Sultzman,"Iroquois History". <http://www.tolatsga.org> (20 Jan. 2002)
&
THE GREAT LAW OF PEACE--variously called: "The Constitution of Iroquois Nations"; "The Great Binding Law - Gayanashagowa"; "Great Law of Peace (untranslated Kaianerakowa)". A document well worth looking at for its own merits, as well as its influence upon Benjamin Franklin and the shaping of

the U.S. Constitution.

"The Origins of the Great Tree of Peace (Peacetree) - The Constitution and Great Law of the Iroquois Nation: The Great Law, Gayanashagowa" Mohawk Nation of Akwesasne - The Origins of the Peacetree. Researched, composed and written by Zoltan E. Szabo, CGA., CFP 1998.
<http://www.peacetree.com/akwesasne/origin.htm> (23 Dec. 2002)

"The Constitution of the Iroquois Nations: The Great Binding Law, Gayanashagowa", Prepared by Gerald Murphy (The Cleveland Free-Net - aa300) Distributed by the Cybercasting Services Division of the National Public Telecomputing Network (NPTN).
<http://www.ku.edu/carrie/docs/texts/iroquois-const.html> (9 Sept.. 2003)

"The Constitution of the Iroquois Nations: The Great Binding Law, Gayanashagowa", National Tribal Justice Resource Center's Tribal Codes and Constitutions - A Project of the National American Court Judges Association , 2002. <http://www.tribalresourcecenter.org/ccfolder/iroquois_const.htm> (9 Sept. 2003)

National Tribal Justice Resource Center's Tribal Codes and Constitutions - A Project of the National American Court Judges Association , 2002 "Tribal Constitutions and By-Laws" (list for numerous tribes)
<http://www.tribalresourcecenter.org/tribalcourts/codes/constdirectory.asp> (9 Sept. 2003)

104 Sultzman, "Iroquois History: <http://www.tolatsga.org/iro.html> (20 Jan. 2002)

Vernon Benjamin, "The Tawagonshi Agreement of 1613 - A Chain of Friendship in the Dutch Hudson Valley" The Hudson Valley Regional Review, 2000 The Bard Center. ("original /real men" and lengthy info. and bibliography <http://www.bard.edu/aboutbard/publications/hvrr/ essays/ tawagonshi/ (6 July 2003)

The Seneca Nation of Indians <http://www.sni.org>

105 "The Sullivan Indian Expedition of 1779: The Aftermath of the Battle of Newtown!", 2000.
<http://thetwintiers.com/generalsullivan/aftermath.htm> (10 Feb.2002)

"Call to Arms: The Iroquois Threat"
<http://thetwintiers.com/generalsullivan/calltoarms.htm> (10 Feb. 2002)

106 Pritchard, *Native New Yorkers,* p. 305.

107 Pritchard, *Native New Yorkers,* ch.17 pp .319-341. (also from Evan T. Pritchard, *No Word For Time: The Way of the Algonquin People, (Appendix).* (San Francisco/Tulsa: Council Oak Books, 1997 (Appendix 2001)). Same info - "The Major Algonquin Nations Throughout North America and What They Call Themselves" <http://www.wilkesweb.net/cac-nations.htm>

108 "A Brief History of New Hampshire", The New Hampshire Almanac - see "Mother of Rivers". (website note: This history was edited and revised from an article in the State of New Hampshire Manual for the General Court 1977, pp. 115-124, published by the New Hampshire Department of State.) <http://www.state.nh.us/nhinfo/history.html> (1 March 2003)

109 Carol B. Smith Fisher, "Who really named Maine?" article from Bangor Daily News, from website "Julie's Genealogy", Julie Sefton, 2001-03.
<http://homepages.rootsweb.com/~julieann/maine_info.htm> (12 Jan. 2003)

110 "Sir Robert Heath's Patent 5 Charles 1st; October, 30 1629", The Avalon Project at Yale Law School - The Colonial Records of North Carolina,

Published under the Supervision of the Trustees of the Public Libraries, by order of the General Assembly. Collected and edited by William L. Saunders, Secretary of State. Vol. I, 1662 to 1712. Raleigh. P. M. Hale, Printer to the State, 1886 (The Colonial Records of North Carolina, Published under the Supervision of the Trustees of the Public Libraries, by order of the General Assembly. Collected and edited by William L. Saunders, Secretary of State. Vol. I, 1662 to 1712. Raleigh. P. M. Hale, Printer to the State, 1886.) Source: The Federal and State Constitutions Colonial Charters, and Other Organic Laws of the States, Territories, and Colonies Now or Heretofore Forming the United States of America. -- Compiled and Edited Under the Act of Congress of June 30, 1906 by Francis Newton Thorpe Washington, DC : Government Printing Office, 1909.
<http://www.yale.edu/lawweb/avalon/heath.htm> (17 March 2002)

[111] James W. Loewen p. 106 *Lies My Teacher Told Me* p.106. (cited as fr. Almon W. Lauber, *Indian Slavery in Colonial Times within the Present Limits of the United States* (Willimastown, Mass.: Corner House, 1970 [1913]) 110. & Lauber, *Indian Slavery in Colonial Times,* 106. Gary Nash, *Red, White, and Black* (Englewood Cliffs, NJ: Prentice-Hall, 1974), 113, 119.)

[112] Jim Powell "William Penn, America's First Great Champion for Liberty and Peace", The Freeman: Ideas on Liberty.
<www.quaker.org/wmpenn.html> (8 March 2003)
"Penn's Holy Experiment: The Seed of a Nation" Quakers and the Political Process: Living our Faith into Action, 2000-01.
<www.pym.org/exhibit/p078.html> (10 March 2003)
Tuomi J. Forrest "Introduction - William Penn, Proprietor"
<http://xroads.virginia.edu/~CAP/PENN/pnintro.html> (8 March 2003)

[113] "Mohawk Trail: History of the Trail"
<http://www.berkshireweb.com/mohawktrail/history/history2/.html>
(25 Juky 2003)

[114] *The American-Heritage® College Dictionary*, Fourth Edition, Boston and New York: Houghton Mifflin Company, 2002.

[115] Miriam Ramirez de Ferrer, M.D. "Puerto Rico's Case before the United Nation's "Committee of 24" " *Puerto Rico Herald* (online), 28 July 2003 "IN 1953, THE UN GENERAL ASSEMBLY RECOGNIZED THAT THE PEOPLE OF PUERTO RICO HAD EFFECTIVELY EXERCISED THEIR RIGHT TO SELF-DETERMINATION AND ACHIEVED A NEW CONSTITUTIONAL STATUS IN A MUTUALLY-AGREED ASSOCIATION WITH THE UNITED STATES WHICH MADE THEM AN AUTONOMOUS POLITICAL ENTITY."
<http://www.puertorico-herald.org/issues/970718/top-story-970718.shtml> (or "search" website) (28 July 2003)
Marisabel Brás, Ph.D. "The Changing of the Guard: Puerto Rico in 1898", 2-21-02, website: The World of 1898: The Spanish American War - Hispanic Division Library of Congress,
<http://www.loc.gov./rr/hispanic/1898/bras.htm> (28 July 2003) or
<http://www.loc.gov./rr/hispanic/> and search

[116] "Declaration of Independence" handwritten 'original' draft.
<http://www.loc.gov/exhibits/treasures/images/decp1.jpg> (12 Feb. 2003)
<http://www.loc.gov/exhibits/treasures/images/uc004215.jpg> (12 Feb. 2003)

[117] Director Herbert Biberman was blacklisted, and as a result his film *Salt of the Earth* (1954) was kept from theaters. The film portrays the true events regarding the harsh conditions of New Mexico mine workers, and is now

considered a classic. I have not seen the film but another excellent film *One of the Hollywood Ten* (2000), portrays the events.

[118] *All the President's Men* movie (1976) Alan J.Pakula, dir., William Goldman, screenplay, based on the book by Carl Bernstein and Bob Woodward (NY: Simon And Schuster, 1974).

[119] a phrase adapted from book title- *Manufacturing Consent: The Political Economy of the Mass Media* by Noam Chomsky and Edward S. Herman, (Pantheon books, 2002.)

[120] William Butler Yeats from his poem "Among School Children"

[121] *The Oxford English Dictionary* "Urano^{-1}"

[122] see also: from ancient Egypt "The Great Hymn to the Aten" and/or "Hymn to the Sun".

[123] Kenneth Yasuda *The Japanese Haiku* (Boston - Rutland, VT - Tokyo: Tuttle Publishing, 1957), p.34.

[124] Johnny Mayer "From 'Beat' to Beatnik" (wesbite note: "This article based on an excellent anthology *The Portable Beat Reader* by Anne Charters.") Blues for Peace Corporation <http://www.bluesforpeace.com/beat.htm> (1 May 2003)

SOURCES CONSULTED and FURTHER READING

AMERICAN INDIAN, AMERICAN HISTORY, LORE
edited by Akwesasne Notes. *basic call to consciousness* Akwesasne Notes, Mohawk Reservation, Via Rooseveltown, NY, 1978.
(history from Hau de no sau nee (Iroquois) perspective. With -Hau de no sau nee Address made in Geneva, Switzerland, 1977, and, Report from Indigenous Peoples from North, Central and South America, also in Geneva, 1977. (This little book has one of the most succinct and enlightening descriptions of history and culture, from an Indian perspective, that I have read.) (parts of this text also at : <http://www.ratical.com/many_worlds/6Nations/6Nations1.html> (27 Dec. 2001)

Brown, Dee. *Bury My Heart At Wounded Knee: An Indian History of the American West* 1970; NY: Holt, Rinehart & Winston, Inc. 1971; Bantam Books 1972.

Brown, Lee - Baha'i-Cherokee. "Native American Indian Prophecies" - excerpts given at the 1986 Baha'i Continental Indigenous Council, Fairbanks, Alaska. <http://www.bci.org/prophecy-fulfilled/nativeam.htm> (2 Oct. 2002)

Loewen, James W. *Lies Across America: What Our Historic Sites Get Wrong* NY: A Touchstone Book, Simon & Schuster, 1999.

Loewen, James W. *Lies My Teacher Told Me: Everything Your American History Textbook Got Wrong* NY: A Touchstone Book, Simon & Schuster, 1995.

Mails, Thomas E. *The Hopi Survival Kit* NY: Penguin / Arkana, 1997.

Nies, Judith *Native American History: A Chronology of a Culture's Vast Achievements and Their Links to World Events* NY: Ballantine Books, a division of Random House, Inc.,1996.

Paine, Thomas. *Common Sense; Rights of Man; The Age of Reason; The Crisis;*

Agrarian Justice.

Peltier, Leonard. - U.S. prisoner #89637-132, Harvey Arden, ed. *Prison Writings: My Life Is My Sun Dance* NY: St. Martin's Griffin, 1999.

Pritchard, Evan T. *Native New Yorkers: The Legacy of the Algonquin People of New York* San Francisco/Tulsa: Council Oak Books, 2002.

Schlosser, Eric. *Fast Food Nation: the dark side of the all-american meal* Boston and New York: Houghton Mifflin Company, 2001.

Toffler, Alvin. *Future Shock* NY: Bantam Books, 1970.

Ventura, Jesse with Mooney, Julie. *Do I Stand Alone?* NY: Pocket Books, a division of Simon & Schuster, 2000.

Vidal, Gore. *The Decline and Fall of the American Empire* Odonian Press, 1986-92.

Vidal, Gore. *Perpetual War for Perpetual Peace: How We Got to Be So Hated* NY: Thunder's Mouth Press/Nation Books, 2002.

Waters, Frank with drawings and source material recorded by Oswald White Bear Fredericks. *Book of the Hopi* Penguin Books, 1963. (Information on the Four Worlds, clans, and migration history.)

Williamson, Marianne. *Healing the Soul of America: Reclaiming Our Voices as Spiritual Citizens* NY: A Touchstone Book publ. by Simon & Schuster, 1991, 2000.

Yaxk'in, Aluna Joy. "Mayan Prophesy The Reawakening Of The Cosmic Human" <http://www.v-j-enterprises.com/mayanpr.html> (25 Aug 2003)

Zinn, Howard. *Declarations of Independence: Cross-Examining American Ideology* NY: HarperPerennial, a Division of HarperCollins Publishers, 1990.

Zinn, Howard. *A People's History of the United States* NY: Perennial Classics, HarperCollins Publishers, 1980.

THE "WORLDS"
O'Bryan, Aileen *"The Dîné: Origin Myths of the Navaho Indians"* Bulletin 163 of the Bureau of American Ethnology of the Smithsonian Institution.[1956] <http://www.sacred-texts.com/nam/nav/omni/omni02.htm> (26 July 2003)

Rahelio. "Harmonic Convergence" <http://www.rahelio.homestead.com/Harmonic_Convergence.html> (30 Aug 2003)

Welker, Glenn. "How the Hopi Indians Reached Their World" site updated 9-9-98 <http://www.indians.org/welker/howtheho.htm> (26 July 2003)

"The Fifth World: A Navajo Legend" as told to Sandoval, Hastin Tlo'tsi Hee, by his grandmother, Esdzan Hosh Kige. Her ancestor was Esdzan at a', the medicine woman who had the Calendar Stone in her keeping. EarthBow, 2001. <http://www.earthbow.com/native/navajo/fifth.htm> (26 July 2003)

"Fifth World" Western Washington University Planetarium, "Starlore of Native America", assembled by Brad Snowder.
<http://www.ac.wwu.edu/~skywise/legends.html> (26 July 2003)
"The Hopi Emergence: The Journey from the First World into the Fourth World" based on "The Four Worlds" from *The Fourth World of the Hopis*. Harold Courlander, University of New Mexico Press, Albuquerque, 1971.
< http://www.hopi.nsn.us/Pages/Culture/emergence.html>

"The Sun, Moon and Stars: A Navajo Traditional Story"
<http://www.kidfox.net/camp/sunmoon.htm> (2 Sept. 2003)

CHINESE
Fazzioli, Edoardo with calligraphy by Rebecca Hon Ko. *Chinese Calligraphy - From Pictograph to Ideogram: The History of 214 Essential Chinese/Japanese Characters* NY-London-Paris: Abbeville Press, 1986.

Ping-gam Go. *Understanding Chinese Characters by their Ancestral Forms*, Third Edition, San Francisco/Larkspur: Simplex Publications,1995.

Sze, Mai-mai. *The Way of Chinese Painting: It's Ideas and Techniques with selections from the Seventeenth Century Mustard Seed Garden Manual of Painting* A Modern Library Paperback (out of print).

Watts, Alan, with collaboration of Al Chung-Liang Hung. *TAO: The Watercourse Way* NY: Pantheon Books, 1975.

Dr. L. Wieger, S.J., trans. into English by L. Davrout, S.J. *Chinese Characters: Their Origin, Etymology, History, Classification and Signification. A Thorough Study From Chinese Documents* NY: Paragon Book Reprint Corp./ NY: Dover Publications, Inc., 1965 (1915 & 1927.)

MUSES
Athena, Ailia "The Muses", *Women in Greek Myths,* 1-8-2002.
<http://www.paleothea.com/SortaSingles/Muses.html> (16 Dec. 2002)

Arrien, Angeles. *The Nine Muses: A Mythological Path to Creativity* NY: Jeremy P. Tarcher/Putnam a member of Penguin Putnam Inc., 2000.

Brewer, Ebenezer Cobham; Adrian Room; Terry Pratchett. *Brewer's Dictionary of Phrase & Fable* , Sixteenth Edition revised by Adrian Room. HarperCollins division of Harper Resource, 1999.

Hesiod. *Theogeny.* trans. Richard Lattimore, in *Hesiod: the Works and Days, Theogeny, the Shield of Herakles* Ann Arbor Paperbacks, 1991, The University of Michigan Press, 1959.

Marks, Tracy *Rediscovering the Muse: Finding Our Personal Source of Inspiration, 1989. <http://www.geocities.com/tmartiac//thalassa/muses2.htm> <http://www.geocities.com/tmartiac//thalassa/muses1.htm> (16 Dec.2002)*

"Carlos Parada, Greek Mythology Link,
http://homepage.mac.com/cparada/GML/" ("Muses") (18 Dec. 2002)

Theoi Project: A Guide To Greek Gods, Spirits and Monsters - "The Mousai (1)"
<http://www.theoi.com/Kronos/Mousai.html> (23 Dec. 2002)

"The Muses and their attributes" Biblioteca del Dipartimento di Astronomia
Pierluigi Battistini, Laura Peperoni e Marina Zuccoli. (on website:
Biblioteca "Guido Horn d'Arturo" del Dipartimento di Astronomia
dell'Università di Bologna e dell'Osservatorio Astronomico di Bologna.)
<http://www.bo.astro.it/~biblio/Vultus-Uraniae/attributes.html>(16 Dec. 2002)

HAIKU
Blyth, R.H. (any of his voluminous books.)

Bowers, Faubion, ed.,*The Classical Tradition of Haiku: An Anthology*
NY: Dover Publications, Inc., NY 1966.
(excellent 3 page forward with concise explanation of haiku.)

Henderson, Harold G. *Haiku in English* Rutland, Vermont & Tokyo, Japan:
Charles E. Tuttle Company, 1967.

Higginson, William J., with Penny Harter. *The Haiku Handbook: How to Write,*
Share, and Teach Haiku NY: Kodansha International, 1985.

Van Den Heuvel, Cor, ed., *The Haiku Anthology: Haiku and Senryu in English*
NY: W.W. Norton & Company, 1999, 3rd ed.
(provides "The Haiku Society of America Definitions".)

Williams, Paul O., Lee Gurga & Michael Dylan Welch, ed., *The Nick of Time:*
Essays on Haiku Aesthetics Foster City, CA: Press Here, 2001.

Yasuda, Kenneth. *The Japanese Haiku: Its Essential Nature, History, and*
Possibilities in English Boston - Rutland, Vermont - Tokyo, Japan:
Tuttle Publishing, 1957.

MYTHOLOGY, POETRY, CLASSICS...
Aristotle. *Poetics.* trans. with intro. and notes Malcolm Heath.
NY: Penguin Books, 1996.

Bruchac, Joseph and Jonathan London, illus. Thomas Locker.
Thirteen Moons on Turtle's Back: A Native American Year of Moons
NY: A PaperStar Book published by The Putnam & Grosset Group,1997.

Deutsch, Babette. *Poetry Handbook: A Dictionary of Terms,* 4th ed.
NY: HarperPerennial a division of HarperCollins Publishers, 1957.
(excellent resource of terms.)

Eddy, Steve. *Native American Myths* UK/USA/Canada: Teach Yourself Books /
Hodder & Stoughton Ltd., 2001.

Homer. *The Odyssey.* trans. Robert Fitzgerald. NY: Farrar, Straus and Giroux,

1962, 1998.

Leeming, David Adams and Margaret Adams Leeming. *A Dictionary of Creation Myths* Oxford/NY: Oxford University Press,1994.

Mason, Herbert. *Gilgamesh: A Verse Narrative.* NY: Mentor publ. by New American Library, a division of Penguin Putnam, Inc., 1970.

Snyder, Gary. *Turtle Island: with "Four Changes"* NY: A New Directions Book, 1969, 1974. (Pulitzer Prize for Poetry 1975)

REFERENCE

The American-Heritage® College Dictionary, Fourth Edition, Boston and New York: Houghton Mifflin Company, 2002.

Merriam-Webster's Collegiate® Dictionary, Tenth Edition, Springfield, Mass: Merriam-Webster, Incorporated, 2000.

The Oxford English Dictionary Clarendon Press, Second Edition,1989.
The Compact Edition of the Oxford English Dictionary Oxford University Press, 1971.

*****

NOTE: "THRERE But For the Grace of God" was first published in the Performance Poets Association™ Literary Review Volume 5, and "we are dumb before the Spirit..." under the title "Communion" in Volume 6.

241

ABOUT THE AUTHOR and PUBLICATIONS
Walter E. Harris III (known to poets and friends as "Mankh")
is a poet and essayist, and a student of Kaballah. He has worked
as an office clerk; house painter; writing instructor; and in various
food service jobs. He enjoys music from around the world, and has
visited or driven through ~36 of the States, plus D.C., Puerto Rico,
and Canada. He lives on Long Island, N.Y.

If you have any further information on 'state names';
Or for other comments,
Or to order books directly:
Please write to: Allbook Books / W. E. Harris III

PO Box 562
Selden, NY 11784

Or email: www.allbook-books.com
             mankh@allbook-books.com

*****

Also available (by the same author) from *Allbook Books*
are two chapbooks of poetry: *Spiral of Life (35 pages)* &
Presence of Birds (34 pages)
They are $6.00 each or $12.00 for both
(shipping and handling included)
&
For more copies of-- *Singing an Epic of Peace*
by mail: $15.00 plus shipping and handling - total $20
money order; or check (allow for clearing delay)

The name *Allbook Books*

honors *Alan*
who was a kind man and a lover of books

*****

242